About Rachel Pollack

Rachel Pollack is a poet, an award-winning novelist, a world authority on the modern interpretation of Tarot cards, and a Tarot card artist. Her novel *Godmother Night* won the 1997 World Fantasy Award. *Unquenchable Fire*, her earlier novel, won the Arthur C. Clarke Award.

Her more than thirty books include twelve books on the Tarot, including *Seventy-Eight Degrees of Wisdom*, often called "the bible of Tarot readers," and she is the creator of the Shining Tribe Tarot. Her books have been published in fourteen languages. Rachel lives in New York's Hudson Valley.

MASTER THE MEANINGS OF THE CARDS

The New
Tarot
HANDBOOK

RACHEL POLLACK

Llewellyn Publications
WOODBURY, MINNESOTA

FIRST EDITION
First Printing, 2011

Author photo by Joyce Tudrin

Book design by Rebecca Zins

Cover background: iStockphoto.com/Peter Zelei

Cover cards (Universal Tarot by Roberto De Angelis)
are used courtesy of Lo Scarabeo

Cover design by Kevin R. Brown

Interior cards are Rider Tarot illustrations based on those
contained in *The Pictorial Key to the Tarot* by Arthur Edward Waite,
published by William Rider & Son Ltd., London, 1911

Llewellyn is a registered trademark
of Llewellyn Worldwide Ltd.

Library of Congress Cataloging-in-Publication Data
Pollack, Rachel, 1945–
  Master the meanings of the cards : the new Tarot handbook / Rachel
Pollack.—1st ed.
      p. cm.
  Includes bibliographical references and index.
  ISBN 978-0-7387-3190-2
  1. Tarot—Handbooks, manuals, etc. I. Title.
  BF1879.T2P643 2012
  133.3′2424—dc23

                                                       2012010380

Llewellyn Publications
A Division of Llewellyn Worldwide Ltd.
2143 Wooddale Drive
Woodbury, MN 55125-2989
www.llewellyn.com
Printed in the United States of America

Dedicated to Johanna Gargiulo-Sherman—teacher, psychic, and creator of the Sacred Rose Tarot— and in memory of Eden Gray.

Special thanks to Barbara Moore, Martha Millard, Zoe Matoff, and the "Becoming a Reader" gang for all their brilliant insights and enthusiasm.

Contents

Introduction

Over the nearly forty-five years of my work with Tarot, people often have asked me how I discovered the cards. To tell the truth, I have learned so much from the cards—spiritual teachings, occult history, psychology, ancient and modern wisdom—it often seems as if the cards discovered *me*. Or maybe they revealed themselves to me when I was ready to receive them.

It happened this way: in early 1970 I was teaching English literature at a college in far northern New York, a very cold place. When a fellow teacher offered to read my Tarot cards if I gave her a ride home, I thought it sounded like a fun idea. I don't remember anything we discussed or what cards came up, only that the cards, and the book my friend used with them, absolutely fascinated me. I knew I had to have them. After some searching in New York City and Montreal, I found both. Of course, this was long before Internet searches, and it was also just before Tarot experienced a great surge in popularity—one that continues to the present day.

I want to say something about that book. It was called *The Tarot Revealed*, and it was by a woman named Eden Gray (isn't that a wonderful name?). The book seemed very simple: a picture and a short text for each card, with instructions on reading, but Gray knew her subject—knew it deeply, with all its hidden wonders—and her book, like the cards themselves, contained far more than it seemed. Around the start of this new century I had the great good fortune to meet Eden Gray. At the age of ninety-six, she was the guest of honor at a large Tarot conference in Chicago. When she was introduced, the entire audience rose to its feet in a great ovation.

For you see, Eden Gray was really the mother of modern Tarot. She told us in Chicago how she had owned a metaphysical bookstore in New York in the 1950s and '60s, and people would ask her for a basic book to learn the cards. She didn't find any, she said, and so she wrote one herself. A few years ago, for a year-long course I was teaching, I decided to trace the history of each card's interpretation. A writer named Paul Huson had compiled lists of early meanings, and I thought it would be valuable to see how ideas about the cards have evolved. I noticed something strange. Some of the modern meanings most readers took for granted did not appear in older commentaries, not even A. E. Waite, whose "Rider Pack" we all followed (for more on this deck, see below). So where did they come from? Finally, I realized: Eden Gray. I also might mention that Gray was the person who first described the Tarot as "the Fool's Journey."

I mention all this because I like to think that this book revives Eden Gray's tradition—a work that is short, direct, yet backed by deeper knowledge and awareness. A work that may open a door or two into Tarot's vast and wonderful storehouse of wisdom and secrets. It is my hope that anyone can use this book to read Tarot—and, in fact, can use it *right away*—but also will find it worth returning to again and again as they themselves become masters of Tarot.

When Eden Gray wrote, and when I began to teach and write about Tarot, we Tarotists believed certain things about the cards that modern research has shown to be historically wrong. For example, most people thought that ordinary playing cards come from the Tarot—a sort of simplified version without the heavily symbolic set of picture cards we now call the Major Arcana. In fact, playing cards came into Europe from North Africa, probably via the Crusaders (*not* the Gypsies) around the end of the fourteenth century. The earliest known Tarot decks appeared some forty to fifty years later, around 1430, in northern Italy, in Ferrara or Milan. To this day, Italian decks are often the most beautiful, the most elegant.

What, then, is a Tarot deck? Simply put, it consists of seventy-eight cards in two parts, the Major Arcana—*arcana* is Latin for secrets—and the four suits of the Minor Arcana. The names of the suits vary, but the most common are Wands, Cups, Swords, and Pentacles. The Majors, also called trumps (from *trionfii*, Latin for triumph), are named and numbered from 0 (the Fool) to 21 (the World), while each suit consists of the same structure, ace through ten, plus four court cards: page, knight, queen, and king.

Modern historians believe, with a good deal of evidence, that the Major Arcana, with its provocative images and titles such as Empress or Devil, did not originally symbolize a secret occult or magical teaching but instead represented the spiritual viewpoint of its time, the early Renaissance. Then, in 1781, something remarkable happened. Two French Freemasons and scholars of the occult, Antoine Court de Gébelin and Count de Mellet, published essays on the Tarot in volume eight of Court de Gébelin's massive history of occult ideas, *Le Monde Primitif* ("The Primitive World"). Together, they outlined a system of ideas and symbols that saw the Tarot as based on Egyptian teachings and the twenty-two letters of the Hebrew alphabet, long believed to have mystical meaning.

These ideas developed all through the nineteenth century until they culminated in a vast synthesis of Tarot, Hebrew letters, Christian mysticism, Pagan gods, astrology, and ritual put together by a secret society of magicians known as the Hermetic Order of the Golden Dawn. For the Golden Dawn, the Tarot is both a grand repository of all knowledge, divine as well as human, and a way to raise yourself to a higher level of being. The original Golden Dawn lasted only some fifteen years, but its influence continues today, as strong as ever.

We do not actually need to study all of this to work with the Tarot, but it is there, supporting us, even if we don't know it. When we read cards, we are, in a sense, putting a great mystical tradition to practical use in our lives.

One of the members of the original Golden Dawn—for a while its leader—was a mystical scholar named Arthur Edward Waite. In the first decade of the twentieth century, Waite decided to create what he called a "rectified" Tarot, one that would embody the symbolic wisdom of the Golden Dawn and his own ideas and insights. To bring his concepts into reality, he hired another Golden Dawn member, a painter, illustrator, and set designer named Pamela Colman Smith, known to her friends as Pixie. (Here's a curious bit of Tarot history: both Waite and Smith were born in Brooklyn, NY, and so was I.)

The deck they created, called the Rider (for its original publisher) or Rider-Waite or RWS (for Rider-Waite-Smith), is the one featured in this book. It is by far the most popular Tarot deck in the world, something that probably would have shocked both Waite and Pixie. What made it such a success was the appearance of people and scenes on the numbered cards of the Minor Arcana. In older decks, the suit cards resemble ordinary playing cards. That is, the Four of Swords simply showed four swords on a white background, the Seven of Cups seven cups, etc. In the Rider we see people doing things like moments in a story. The result is a kind of kaleidoscope of life experiences. While the Major Arcana represents large principles, the Minor cards give us a more immediate sense of challenges and victories, sorrows and joys.

Though this book, like almost all Tarot books, describes the cards in order, the deck is meant to be shuffled, so that we constantly rearrange it, constantly create new possibilities. And even though we assign meanings to each card, its true power really comes alive when we see it in answer to a question in a reading. Thus the Tarot, and what we can learn from it, is truly inexhaustible. The meaning of the Lovers seems clear when we ask "What can I expect from this relationship?" (good news!), but suppose it comes up in answer to the question "How should I approach the meeting with my boss?" (It's probably *not* telling you to seduce him.) In this book I have tried to guide you into the cards with information about the symbolism and meaning of each one. The best way to learn the Tarot, however, is to use it.

Some people believe you should never try to read the cards until you have gone through the book, studied it, even memorized the meanings of all seventy-eight pictures, both upright and reversed. Others believe you shouldn't even look at the explanations in a book until you have explored the cards on your own, guided by sensitivity and intuition. Whatever approach works for you is the one you should follow. However, here is what I did: I got the deck and I got Eden Gray's book, and I read the instructions for laying out a reading. For each card, I would set it down, consider it, then look it up in the book. Rather than read through the descriptions ahead of time and try to remember them, I got to know the cards in practice. In the process I did readings, mostly for my friends, that astonished both me and them with what the cards revealed.

At the same time that I checked the book for each card, I did not hesitate to go beyond what *any* book described if my intuition told me it was something different. I gave myself this freedom for two reasons. First, the descriptions were basic, and clearly we need to adapt them to each situation. Second, I could see just looking at the cards that they contained whole worlds of wisdom beyond what any book could explain.

So, if you wish to read through this book before you read the cards, by all means do so. And if you want to find your own way through the pictures before you venture past the introduction, go ahead. And if you want to start reading the cards right away, with the deck in one hand and this book in the other, I invite you to start.

You will notice that each of the sections on the Major Arcana contains a description of the card and its symbolism, a set of upright and reversed meanings (reversed just means that when you turn a card face up, the picture appears upside down), and then, perhaps a little unusually, a spread, or layout, inspired by each card. Each Major card really presents its own unique view of the world, so that when we do one of these readings (using the whole deck) it's as if we ourselves become the Magician or the Empress or the Fool asking about magic or passion or foolishness in our lives. Some of these spreads first appeared in my book *Tarot Wisdom,* but they go back much further. Many were created for a year-long course I taught called "Becoming a Reader," but really, they come from my more than forty years reading—and playing—with the Tarot.

For nearly half a century I have worked with the Tarot, read it, thought about it, studied and played with it. After all this time, I can say one thing with certainty: we will never come to the end of it. The Tarot grows and changes as we grow and change. Let the Tarot discover you so that you may discover yourself in the cards.

· · · · · ·

The
Major Arcana

The Major Arcana is what makes Tarot Tarot. This is true both as a simple fact—we define Tarot as a deck with four suits and the twenty-two cards of the Major Arcana—and on deep levels of meaning. No one knows exactly when people started to tell fortunes with ordinary playing cards, but I suspect the practice probably goes back almost to the introduction of cards, since just about every device or game people use for gambling also gets used in divination (and many other things, of course; no one gambles with bird entrails or the holes in cheese, both of which have been used for divination). Reading cards, then, is not something unique to Tarot. But when we read with Tarot it's the Major Arcana that gives our readings layers of understanding beyond the simple answers to our questions. In fact, this is true even if no Major Arcana cards happen to show up in the reading, for in the Tarot the Minor Arcana cards resonate with the symbolic ideas of the Majors.

The first card sets with "triumphs," or trumps, the original name for the Major Arcana, appeared around 1430 in Italy. As described in the introduction, people have long argued over whether those first trumps formed some kind of secret doctrine and, if so, what that doctrine might be. The fact is, it doesn't matter. If the trumps did not originally portray Egyptian teachings or the Jewish mystical tradition known as Kabbalah, they have *always* carried spiritual messages. With such figures as a female pope (the High Priestess in modern decks), alchemist Hermits, with angels (Temperance, the Lovers) and a Devil, or death and resurrection (Judgement), they invite us to look at our own lives, and the world around us, in meaningful ways.

Ever since 1781 and those first occult theories of ancient Egyptian origins, the Major Arcana has become more and more structured, more and more a coherent story. Names have changed, pictures have become transformed, and symbols added, all to bring about that deep and subtle story.

Eden Gray called it "the Fool's Journey," and the name has stuck ever since. The Fool represents the soul, who travels from birth through life's various challenges, to death and even beyond, to spiritual enlightenment. The wonderful thing about this grand tale is that at every stage we can adapt it to valuable messages for our own lives, right now. This is what we do in readings: take these deeply symbolic pictures and apply them to a specific issue or situation. At the same time, those larger meanings don't go away. Thus, in a reading, say, about a problem with your sister-in-law, the cards will subtly connect you to important teachings even if you don't quite realize it. This is part of what makes Tarot special—what makes it Tarot. Since the card descriptions can become complex, I have begun with keywords and ended with suggested divinatory and reversed meanings.

How, then, can we understand this tale of the Fool on his journey? Because twenty-one "chapters" can seem cumbersome, we usually divide the cards into groups. For example, we might think of cards 1 through 10 as the first half of the story, 11 through 20 as the second half, with the World card, 21, as the climax. This allows us to make some interesting comparisons between the first and second halves:

$$1 \quad 2 \quad 3 \quad 4 \quad 5 \quad 6 \quad 7 \quad 8 \quad 9 \quad 10$$

Fool (0) World (21)

$$11 \quad 12 \quad 13 \quad 14 \quad 15 \quad 16 \quad 17 \quad 18 \quad 19 \quad 20$$

Or we can look at 1 through 10 as the first half, 12 through 21 as the second, with the balanced scales of Justice as the pivotal moment between the two parts:

Fool (0)

$$1 \quad 2 \quad 3 \quad 4 \quad 5 \quad 6 \quad 7 \quad 8 \quad 9 \quad 10$$

Justice (11)

$$12 \quad 13 \quad 14 \quad 15 \quad 16 \quad 17 \quad 18 \quad 19 \quad 20 \quad 21$$

For myself, I have found it valuable—and simpler—to divide the Major Arcana into the Fool plus three lines of seven.

Fool (0)

$$1 \quad 2 \quad 3 \quad 4 \quad 5 \quad 6 \quad 7$$

$$8 \quad 9 \quad 10 \quad 11 \quad 12 \quad 13 \quad 14$$

$$15 \quad 16 \quad 17 \quad 18 \quad 19 \quad 20 \quad 21$$

Three and seven are not arbitrary numbers. Images of three are found over and over in the world's mythologies and religious teachings. There is the Christian trinity of Father-Son-Holy Spirit, the Hindu *trimurti* of Creator-Preserver-Destroyer, and the European Triple Goddess of Maiden-Mother-Crone, connected to the phases of the moon but also to the three Fates who determine our lives. In modern philosophy we find the idea of thesis-antithesis-synthesis. To my way of thinking, all these come from one of the most basic facts of our existence: that we each combine the genes of a mother and a father, so father-mother-child is the original trinity.

And seven? Remember that of those ten astrological "planets," seven could be seen with the naked eye. This is, in fact, why we have seven days in the week, each one "ruled" by a planetary energy. We also find seven colors in the rainbow, seven primary chakras (energy centers) in the human body, and seven notes in the musical scale (*do, re, mi, fa, so, la, ti,* and then starting over again with *do*).

In America, people used to be considered adults only when they reached the age of twenty-one, the same number as the cards in the Major Arcana.

Three lines of seven. Three stages of the Fool's Journey. We could describe the first as the outer challenges of life—growing up, dealing with parents and society, learning to love, creating a successful life. This stage culminates in the strong-willed, confident Chariot. Part two of the story takes the Fool through a profound transformation, beginning with the gentleness of Strength and the mysterious light of the Hermit, and ending with the Death of everything that once seemed so important in order for the Fool—for *us*—to discover what I call our true "angelic" selves in card 14, Temperance.

The Fool has come so far, even died and been reborn, and yet seven more cards remain—a whole other level. Here the Fool becomes a true mythic hero, for while these final cards may seem very complicated, they actually tell a very simple tale, what I call the Liberation of Light. Darkness in the Devil (card 15), then a flash of lightning in the Tower (card 16), followed by the ever-increasing light of Star, Moon, and Sun (cards 17, 18, and 19), until at last we come to the glory of Judgement and the perfection of the World.

What wondrous tales! As well as the three horizontal rows—1 through 7, 8 through 14, and 15 through 21—we can look at seven vertical rows; for example, 1, 8, and 15 (Magician, Strength, and Devil) or 7, 14, and 21 (Chariot, Temperance, and World). A Tarotist named Caitlín Matthews referred to these as "triads," and we shall look at some of them as we make our way through the cards.

And, finally, what does all this have to do with readings? Isn't that why most people turn to the cards—why we first became interested? All this talk of mythic journeys may be exciting, but will it help us figure out how to find our soul mate? Well, yes. One thing it will do is help us understand just what a "soul mate" might mean and where this idea comes from. More generally, the best meanings for the cards derive from their symbolic truths. Too often in the past, people who've gone deeply into the Tarot's wisdom considered the practice of readings irrelevant or even insulting. As result, their lists of divinatory meanings may simply repeat old formulas, without any connection to the actual pictures. This can make the meanings trivial and hard to use in readings. For my own descriptions I have tried to let the meanings grow naturally out of the cards' images, stories, and spiritual wonders—that, and my own forty-plus years as a Tarot reader.

· · · · · · ·

THE FOOL.

KEYWORDS:
freedom, risk, young in spirit, immature

One of the most famous figures in the Tarot, he stands or dances on what seems to be the edge of a cliff. Will he step off? And if he does, will he fall or will the folds of his bright tunic catch the wind and let him soar? He himself appears unconcerned as he tilts his head up to the light. A little dog—white for purity, like the white sun above his head—capers beside him, as carefree and joyous as its master. Some say the dog is his animal instinct warning him of danger—what do you think?

The essence of this card lies not in the picture but in its number, 0. The shape of an egg, out of which a new life will emerge, zero signifies freedom, unattachment, the chance to do something new—maybe to let go of the past and start over. Even more, the idea of nothing, *no-thing*, reminds us that we are not all the labels and judgments other people put on us, or even the ones we put on ourselves. We cannot be pinned down, limited, dismissed. Remember in school when you learned that if you divide any number by zero, the answer is always infinity? Take any situation that limits or blocks you, including your own beliefs about yourself, then bring in the Fool, and suddenly there are limitless—infinite—possibilities.

Many people see the Fool as the "hero" of the Tarot, the figure who travels through all the other cards until he becomes transformed in the World. The wreath around the woman in the World is shaped like a zero/egg. The two cards, 0 and 21, the beginning and the end, are the only cards where we see someone dancing. Except for the people falling from the Tower, all the others stand or sit. Eden Gray, remember, called the Tarot "the Fool's Journey," a phrase many have echoed ever since. Some eighty years earlier, A. E. Waite, designer of the card, wrote that "he is a prince of the other world on his travels through this one."

Notice the bag he carries on a stick over his shoulder, like an old-time hobo. Some say it contains his life experiences, others his memories of past lives. Either way, he bears them lightly and does not mistake them for his true self, which, after all, is nothing. In his hat he wears a scarlet feather, symbol of passionate freedom. We will see the same feather in the hair of the Sun child.

We'd all like to be the Fool—sometimes. Act spontaneously, without doubt or fear. Not care what anyone thinks of us. Not worry about what happens next. But would you want to act so freely all the time? What about jobs, relationships, family? As with every card, there are times when the Fool is exactly what we need and others when planning or caution is necessary. The position in the reading, and the other cards, can help us understand how to interpret it.

· · · · · ·

DIVINATORY MEANINGS:

Freedom, spontaneity, recklessness. Acting on instinct rather than plans or thought. All things are possible. Taking a chance on love or new ideas. Setting out.

REVERSED:

Caution, maturity, anxiety. Need for planning before an action. Sometimes overly cautious. Can be losing touch with your instincts.

A READING FOR
The Fool

```
                    1

        2           3

        4           5

                6
```

1. How have I been a Fool in my life?

2. How has it helped me?

3. How has it hurt me?

4. Where in my life do I need to be more foolish?

5. Where will the Fool *not* serve me?

6. What gifts does the Fool bring me?

THE MAGICIAN.

KEYWORDS:
creativity, magic, active principle

He stands in a bower of life, surrounded by red roses (for passion) and white lilies (for purity). The same two colors appear in his robes, the red of desire cloaking the white of pure intention and power without selfishness. The crystal-like magic wand in his right hand points up toward the heavens, as if it draws down the energy of the gods. But the energy is not for himself, for his left hand points down to the flowers. He is a servant of creation. Energy moves through him, and he directs it but does not try to control it or hold on to it. This experience of flowing energy is not reserved for great magicians. Artists know it, and so do scientists, teachers, athletes. Ask any painter or writer, and they will all say the same thing: "When it's going well, it's like *I'm* not doing it, something is doing it through me. I just have to get out of the way."

Getting out of the way is not enough; we also need mastery, and craft, and dedication. The Magician represents a high level of attainment in whatever a person is doing. On the table before him lie the four emblems of the Minor Arcana, the wand (flowering stick), the cup, the sword, and the pentacle. They show he has learned to focus and direct the four elements of life: Fire, Water, Air, and Earth. Everything works together under the guidance of a strong and dedicated will.

As card 1, the Magician represents singleness of purpose, awareness, action. He is the light of consciousness, compared to the High Priestess's intuitive darkness. He also signifies the pure masculine, just as the High Priestess is the pure feminine. This does not mean the Magician is only for men or the High Priestess is only for women. We all experience each of these principles at different times and in our own way. Reading cards can help us see the shifting energies of our lives. In fact, this is one of the main reasons to do it.

In Roman numerals the number 1 is I, and the Magician may symbolize the ego. But there is no vanity in him. Instead, the I represents the self united with higher purpose. Above his head we see the infinity sign, called a lemniscate in Tarot tradition (found also on the cards of Strength and the Two of Pentacles). Around his waist he wears a snake with its tail in its mouth, an ancient symbol of eternity. The infinite and the eternal—neither means "a very long time" or even "endless." Rather, they are something we experience in special moments.

One of those might be when you do a reading and the truth of the cards flows through you, true and clear.

His posture of one arm up, one arm down symbolizes the great esoteric principle "as above, so below." The lemniscate, a sideways figure eight, reminds us to add "as within, so without." Our lives, which may appear random, disconnected, or meaningless, are connected to the great, flowing patterns of life. The lemniscate also may remind us of something we learned in high school physics: energy cannot be created or destroyed. The events in our lives reflect the inner truth of who we are.

Do you want to know the best way to actually experience these principles? Read Tarot cards.

· · · · · ·

DIVINATORY MEANINGS:

Consciousness, light, creativity, transformation. Masculine energy in its best sense. Magic, however we may understand it, is present right now in our lives. As card 1, it can signify a positive beginning to a new project or a new phase in a person's life. Singleness of will aligned with a higher purpose. It's time to make the right decision and take action.

REVERSED:

Blocked energy, which can result in feelings of weakness or misuse of power. There may be a need to realign yourself with what is pure and true in your life. There may be something you need to do or some decision you need to make. You might ask yourself, "Do I doubt myself too much? How can I serve a higher purpose?"

A READING FOR
The Magician

1

2   3

4   5

1. What does magic mean to me?

2. How does magic act in my life?

3. Where do I look for it?

4. How do I find it?

5. How do I use it?

THE HIGH PRIESTESS

KEYWORDS:
wisdom, intuition, stillness

She sits between two pillars, light and darkness, with a rolled-up scroll in her lap to hide her secrets. Where the Magician communicates, she is silent. Where the Magician lets energy pour through him into action and creativity, the Priestess contains her wisdom. Unlike the Hierophant, or High Priest, who gives out rules and teachings, the High Priestess sits alone, without disciples. Her scroll is marked "Tora," but unlike the Jewish Torah, read in synagogues every Saturday morning, her law remains unopened and undisplayed, for the truth she knows cannot be broken down into words and explanations. Have you ever felt you understood something beyond language, something so deep that if you tried to spell it out for someone it would become meaningless? That is the High Priestess.

Originally called Papesse, or female pope (just as the Hierophant is called the Pope in European decks), she represents feminine spiritual power balancing the dominance of an all-male priesthood (and the habit of referring to God as "he"). As vital as that is, however, she signifies something more—the very embodiment of mystery. The B and J on her pillars identify them as Boaz and Jachin, the columns that stood at the entrance to Solomon's Temple in ancient Jerusalem. Notice that, like the Chinese yin-yang symbol, the dark pillar contains a white letter and the light, a black one. If we find this moment of perfect stillness, of clarity beyond words, we know that every situation contains the seeds of its opposite.

She wears the robes of the goddess Isis, known in the ancient world as the Goddess with a Thousand Names. Her foot rests on a crescent moon, while her crown is actually the moon's phases—the horns on either side represent the waxing and waning moon, with the circle in the middle as the full moon.

The curtain behind her bears pomegranates in circles of light. This voluptuous fruit, filled with life-giving juice, multiple seeds, and even a plant variety of estrogen, links her to the goddess Persephone, a mover between the world of the living and the land of the dead (see the Empress and the Star). The pomegranate also connects her to Kabbalah, the Jewish and later Christian/esoteric mystical tradition so bound up with Tarot. The Kabbalists sometimes describe spiritual paradise as *pardes rimonim*, an orchard of pomegranates. And the pattern of the pomegranates suggests the map of consciousness known as the tree of life (for the full pattern, see the Ten of Pentacles).

Does all this symbolism require vast learning before we try to understand the card? Look carefully at the gaps between the pillars and the curtain, and you will see what lies beyond her: water. Not some secret temple, not a mountain of scholarly books, just still water, the image of peace and depth. She is the priestess of wisdom, not information. The Tarot *invites* us to learn its complex symbols, but it does not require us to study or memorize.

• • • • • •

DIVINATORY MEANINGS:

A time for silence and stillness rather than activity. Trusting your intuition, being with yourself. Sensing mysteries and truths that do not need to be explained. Sometimes a style of leadership that helps others find their own way rather than giving them directions.

REVERSED:

The need to get involved in outer activities or be with people. Communication; sharing ideas and knowledge. There may be a need to express passion or take a stand or commit to something. In some situations it may indicate pressure from other people.

A READING FOR
The High Priestess

1   2

3

4   5

1. What is deep within me?

2. How can I know it?

3. How can I be true to it?

4. What do I need to give to others?

5. What do I need to keep within?

THE EMPRESS.

KEYWORDS:
passion, love, motherhood, abundance

The first five cards of the Major Arcana constantly pair up with each other. The Magician and High Priestess represent basic principles of light and darkness, action and stillness, male and female. But the Priestess also goes with the Priest, the Hierophant. The Empress and the Emperor are clearly a couple, but so are the Emperor and the Magician, for each symbolizes a dynamic masculine energy. And the Emperor and the Hierophant together set rules and teachings. As for the Empress and the Magician, the Golden Dawn linked the Empress to Venus, known to the Greeks as Aphrodite, and the Magician to Mercury, whom the Greeks called Hermes. Together the two names form hermaphrodite, the perfect blend of male and female.

Yet another pair are the High Priestess and the Empress—two aspects of the female: the self-contained, virginal Priestess and the outgoing, passionate Empress. Notice that unlike the Lovers card, with its graceful couple, the Empress does not have a partner. Her love goddess sexuality is about her own life energy, not her relationships. Her passion flows into all she does, like the waterfall that pours into the stream flowing underneath her throne.

Her twelve-starred crown, for the twelve signs of the zodiac, reveals her as a Queen of Heaven. The High Priestess can be seen as Mary the Virgin, the Empress as Mary the Mother. Thus in a reading she may represent actual motherhood or pregnancy. Some people see the picture as showing a pregnant woman. Take a look and decide for yourself.

As well as the star crown of the Queen of Heaven, she bears symbols of two goddesses. The woman symbol on her heart-shaped shield is actually the sign of Venus/Aphrodite, that ruler of passionate, unstoppable love. The wheat that grows around her identifies her as Demeter, the goddess of plants and agriculture, and the symbol of devoted motherhood. Demeter's daughter, Persephone (see the High Priestess and the Star), was taken by Hades, ruler of the dead, to be his bride in the underworld.

When Demeter wailed for her lost child, the gods told her not to complain. Hades made the perfect husband, they said: untold wealth and a never-ending stream of worshippers. Demeter refused to give in. She stopped the plants from growing until Zeus, king of the gods, ordered Hades to return Persephone. The moral of this great story? Never underestimate a mother!

Aphrodite and Demeter—two sides of the passionate feminine. We can only add one of the Tarot's most important lesson, taught to us by reading the cards. The Empress is not just for women. If a man gets this card, it can mean his mother or his lover or his wife, but it also may refer to the man's own expression of passion or devotion.

· · · · · ·

DIVINATORY MEANINGS:

Passion, emotion. Love of life, of nature. It may indicate the querent's mother or the querent as a mother. Sometimes (with other cards) pregnancy. Satisfaction, pleasure, sensuality.

REVERSED:

Thoughtfulness, caution, the intellect rather than the senses. Can be problems with a domineering or harsh mother, or possibly difficulties getting pregnant.

A READING FOR
The Empress

```
        1   2   3

      4   5   6

      7   8   9
```

1. What is my passion?

2. How have I expressed it?

3. How can I express it more fully?

4. What blocks me?

5. What frees me?

6. What do I nurture?

7. What does nurturing ask of me?

8. What does it give me?

9. How can I bring together my passion
   and my nurturance?

THE EMPEROR.

KEYWORDS:
rules, structures, fatherhood, society

The fact that the Empress comes before the Emperor reflects an ancient viewpoint that the male is the consort of the female. That is, not only does the father provide the seed to the mother who grows the baby, but also, most of us know our mothers more intimately than we do our fathers. And if we look beyond the family, nature comes before society. Where the Empress represents the image of the loving, all-embracing Mother, the Emperor takes the role of the strong, sometimes harsh Father. Where she is the endless fertility of nature, he symbolizes the rules and structure of our social world. The Emperor can signify government, laws, power, civilization itself.

It is easy to see him as hard and cold, sitting on his throne in a desert, body covered in armor, with sharp, lifeless mountains lined up behind him. The Empress's surging waters that gushed from a waterfall to flow beneath her throne here become a narrow stream just managing to cut its way through the stone cavern. And, in fact, many people do dislike this card, often more than, say, the Devil. But without the structures of society, how would we survive? Many of us love the time we spend in nature, but we would not like it if we had to build our own homes or hunt and gather our own food.

The Emperor may signify a person's actual father or being a father, with all its responsibilities. As we have seen with other cards, these Emperor qualities can appear for a woman. When women structure their lives or lay down rules or defend something of value or take a strong position on something, they can become the Emperor. Smith drew this card as fearsome and cold—that armor rules out loving embraces!—as if we are children looking at an angry father and his scowl and threat of punishment. There is something infantile about the way we often see this card. But if we learn to see ourselves as powerful and are willing to set rules or defend what matters to us, then the card becomes exhilarating.

In Tarot numerology the Fool becomes card 22, and 2+2=4, the Emperor. The two cards are linked by being polar opposites—the Fool the carefree child who wants to dance, the Emperor with his commitment to rules and responsibilities. As 0, the Fool does not even try to limit himself. As 4, the

Emperor becomes like the four solid walls of a house. Does the Fool have more fun? Probably. But we tend to look at the Emperor from outside. What might it be like to experience his power or that ability to take charge of your life?

. . . . . .

DIVINATORY MEANINGS:

Society, authority, responsibility. Rules, government, a boss or someone in power. The querent's father or the querent being or becoming a father. Taking charge of your life or defending something important.

REVERSED:

Immaturity, freedom from responsibilities. Gentleness. A loving parent, especially a kind or benevolent father. Alternatively (especially with one or more reversed kings), a misuse of authority.

A READING FOR
The Emperor

1   2   3

4   5   6

1. How am I an Emperor in my life?

2. How am I *not* an Emperor?

3. Where do I need to take charge?

4. How am I weak?

5. How am I strong?

6. What rules, conscious or unconscious, govern my life?

THE HIEROPHANT

KEYWORDS:
tradition, conformity, spiritual blessings

The original name for this card is the Pope, and that remains the image—a crowned pope on his throne with two monks kneeling before him. The title "Hierophant" comes from the ancient Mystery schools dedicated to secret teachings and spiritual initiations. *Hierophant* means the one who shows, or reveals, the sacred objects and their hidden meanings. Thus, the monks do not simply bow to authority, they give themselves to blessings and wisdom.

Like the Magician, but also the Devil (the Devil's number, 15, consists of 1, the Magician, and 5, the Hierophant), he raises his right arm. Instead of raising a wand, like the Magician, he makes a gesture—two fingers up, two down—which is an actual priestly blessing. It also symbolizes the great dictum "as above, so below," that our own small lives belong to a larger pattern, and our individual actions carry meaning. The Hierophant acts as a bridge (the pope's title, *pontiff*, means "bridge") between higher and lower worlds.

Churches and priests of all religions do not just transmit blessings, they also teach rules and morality and traditional ideas of how to act and even think. They often expect the rest of us to obey them. Thus, the monks bow before the Hierophant's authority. Many people dislike this card, especially those who have rebelled against some strict religious upbringing, with threats of Hell if they did not do as they were told. Along with the previous card, the Emperor, the Hierophant can signify authority or a path laid out for you that everyone expects you to follow. Examples might be going to the right school (instead of taking off to see the world, like the Fool), working in the family business, marrying a "good match," and having babies; we can all supply our own examples, whether we followed them or rebelled against them.

Because priests marry people, the card can signify marriage. Without such cards as the Empress, the Lovers, or the Four of Wands, the Hierophant may indicate a marriage less about love than about all the laws and rules and expectations of being married. If the card shows up in a reading about a new and exciting relationship, it may hint that the person is married, especially if the Seven of Swords also appears.

The Hierophant is the first in a large group of cards with a three-part image—that is, one figure above two others. Here we see the Hierophant and his two monks. Next comes the angel blessing the man and woman in the Lovers, then the Charioteer standing above the two sphinxes. Not every card follows this, but we find it in many, including such Minor Arcana cards as the Six of Pentacles, with the merchant above the two beggars. For each of these we might see the dominant figure in the middle as holding together the different aspects of life. Here it's tradition and spiritual teachings, but also conformity to religious laws and other people's expectations.

· · · · · ·

DIVINATORY MEANINGS:

Spiritual teachings and laws. Education in general.
Conformity, following a path laid out for you by social
roles or family expectations. Blessings, possibly marriage.

REVERSED:

Nonconformity, rebellion, making your own way. Original
thinking but also can suggest gullibility. Possibly a cult.

A READING FOR
The Hierophant

1

4   5

2   3

1. How has tradition affected my life?

2. What have I learned?

3. How have I broken with tradition?

4. What do I have to teach others?

5. How can I fulfill this role?

THE LOVERS.

relationship, love, choice to be made

Along with Death and the Fool (and the entire Minor Arcana!), this is one of the most dramatic of the Rider deck's changes from the traditional Tarot. The old version, often labeled the Lover (singular), or just Love, showed a young man between two women, as if he must choose between them. One allegorical interpretation sees the women as Vice and Virtue, and the choice a moral one. At the same time, he's young, and above him, Cupid (not an angel in the older decks) is about to shoot an arrow at him, reminding us that sometimes we make choices based on desire and feeling—and hormones.

In the sequence of cards, the Lovers, next to last in the first group of seven, can represent adolescence. The Fool—the soul on its journey through life—encounters the great archetypes of masculine and feminine energies in the Magician and High Priestess, grows up with Mommy and Daddy (the Empress and Emperor), and learns the traditions of his culture in the Hierophant. But these are all things outside us. In adolescence we first begin to have our own experiences as we separate from our parents and teachers. We do this emotionally, often intellectually, sometimes morally, choosing different values than our parents and teachers. Most of all, however, we make our own romantic and sexual choices, driven by hormones and our unique personalities.

In the Rider image we see, instead of adolescent choice, the image of a deep love—and not just any couple. The figures are Adam and Eve standing before the tree of life and the tree of knowledge. There is a significant difference from the biblical story we all know. They are not shown as sinful or fallen but idealized. In the traditional story, God expels the couple from Eden and sets an angel with a flaming sword to guard the gate so they cannot slip back in. Here the archangel Raphael unites and blesses them. *Rapha-el* means "healing power of God," and so the message of this card is that love heals.

The card shows Adam and Eve as they should have been, without corruption, and thus a model of the ideal relationship, a union of spirit as well as desire. We also might see all three figures together as a model of the self. The man symbolizes the rational mind, the woman the emotional. Adam looks to

Eve, who looks up to the higher self of the angel, whose out-stretched arms bless them. In other words, the rational mind cannot reach a higher state unless it travels through feelings.

There is an interesting game we can play with the first six numbers of the Major Arcana. If we add 1 and 2, the basic archetypes of Magician and High Priestess, we get the Empress, nature. If we add $1+2+3$, male and female joined by passion, we get 6, the Lovers. If we bring in the Emperor's rules, $1+2+3+4=10$, the Wheel of Fortune, the laws of fate and karma. Add 5, the Hierophant's doctrines, and we find the Devil (and who talks more about Hell than priests?). But if we then add the Lovers, $1+2+3+4+5+6=21$, the World, the culmination of the Major Arcana, symbol of spiritual attainment. Love is the ultimate salvation.

- - - - - -

DIVINATORY MEANINGS:

Love, a deep relationship, choices, desire. Good partnership in business or creative work. The rational and the emotional in harmony with each other.

REVERSED:

Not a time for relationships, especially if it appears with the Hermit or the High Priestess. Difficulties in a marriage or relationship. Conflict between emotions and ideas or values.

A READING FOR
The Lovers

1   2

5   6

3   4

1. How have I experienced love in my life?

2. What has come from it?

3. What do I desire?

4. What holds me back?

5. What does love ask of me?

6. What can love give me?

THE CHARIOT.

KEYWORDS:

will, success, power

The Chariot gives us the first of three "victory" cards, each of which end a sequence of seven—7, the Chariot; 14, Temperance; and 21, the World. Here the victory is over the outer challenges of life to become a successful person. The Fool has grown up, maybe moved to the city and gotten his first (2 sphinxpower) chariot. If we look at a wider perspective, we might remember that in ancient times, heroes or kings rode in chariots through the city the way our modern heroes—sports champions, astronauts, and sometimes national leaders—will be driven in open-air limousines past cheering crowds.

We can see symbolic references to each of the previous six cards, as if the Fool has taken them all into himself. He holds a wand like the Magician's, only longer, and the crescent moons on his shoulders recall the High Priestess. Like the famous stage masks of tragedy and comedy, one crescent smiles, the other frowns, to represent the variety of life experiences. The starry canopy, as well as the star crown, recall the Empress's zodiac tiara, while the square block of the chariot itself and the city behind him suggest the Emperor's firm structure of law and society. The black-and-white sphinxes may remind us of the Hierophant's disciples as well as the pillars of the High Priestess. Most subtly we find the Lovers in what looks like a nut-and-bolt image on the front of the Chariot. This is an Indian symbol called a lingam and yoni, the lingam/rod of the Hindu god Shiva penetrating the womb/yoni of the goddess Shakti.

This is the third of three cards in a row that show us one figure over two others—the Hierophant with his two monks, the angel blessing the Lovers, and now the Charioteer standing firmly above the crouching sphinxes, whose colors symbolize the oppositions and contradictions of life. No reins hold them in check; the Charioteer uses focused will to keep them together. His power and success do not come from outside titles or social approval but from his own ability to direct his energy and make his life what he envisions. And yet, he does not actually resolve the contradictions. Can he hold things together through will alone?

The square, gray body of the Chariot may symbolize the material world. Has he gotten stuck in his success? We need the Fool's dancing freedom in such moments, to leave our victories and open ourselves to the next part of the journey. The white square on his chest symbolizes matter. Temperance, the card below him in the seventh triad, displays a triangle in a square—the spiritual within the physical—while the third card, the World, shows a woman dancing in an egg-shaped victory wreath.

Between the masks of sadness and happiness on his shoulders, his face appears impassive. Has he risen above the universal tendency to swing back and forth between highs and lows? Or is he simply wearing another mask?

. . . . . .

DIVINATORY MEANINGS:

Success in the world, strong will, achievement, the respect of others. The tendency to show a calm exterior and keep feelings inside. On a very literal level, travel, maybe even a new car.

REVERSED:

Weak will, delays or setbacks, difficulty holding together contradictions. Sometimes allowing your true feelings to show or the freedom of leaving something behind. Canceled trip or even car trouble.

A READING FOR
The Chariot

0

1

3   4

7

5   6

2

The positions in this spread are based on the first eight cards of the Major Arcana. If a card comes up in its own position—say, the Emperor in position four—its power is emphasized.

0, Fool. What am I leaping into at this time in my life?

1, Magician. Where is the energy, the magic?

2, High Priestess. What is secret or hidden or unspoken?

3, Empress. What is my passion?

4, Emperor. What are the rules I follow (possibly hidden or unconscious)?

5, Hierophant. What is the path laid out for me?

6, Lovers. How do I express my passion?

7, Chariot. Where is it all heading?

KEYWORDS:
*personal strength, transforming negativity,
emotional openness*

More than any other card, when Strength comes up in a reading, we need to ask the querent (or ourselves) what the word means. What does it mean to be strong? For that is what this card, at its most basic, is telling you: that you have (or need) strength, also called fortitude, one of the four cardinal virtues. But this virtue can mean many different things.

For many it is an inner belief in yourself. For others it's what allows you to do the right thing or to continue on a difficult path. In the Middle Ages it meant overcoming animal desire or passion. Some early images showed Hercules clubbing the Nemean lion to death, the first of his famous twelve tasks, as if we can beat our lower desires into submission (sadly, people have beaten children for just that reason).

The Virtues were often depicted as women, and so the image changed to a woman subduing a lion, more with gentleness and confidence than aggression. It's worth noting that in a deck famous for its androgynous figures, the woman who represents fortitude appears as one of the most feminine, even more so than the Empress. She subdues the lion by caressing him, taming him with her touch, so that he almost resembles a puppy with his tail between his legs. The Chariot shows us the power of masculine will to overcome life's challenges. Here we see a feminine Strength that tames rather than subdues.

Three cards in the Major Arcana show a human and animal in close relationship—the Fool with his dog, Strength with her lion, and the Sun child on his horse. In each case the animal nature becomes a partner to the human consciousness, but in Strength they seem the closest.

The juncture between the Chariot and Strength forms one of those places where we most need the Fool's willingness to leave behind everything that is known and take the next step. For what could be more foolish than to give up success and accomplishment and the admiration of the outside world for a strange inner journey in a world that leads to death and transformation?

She wears what appears to be a belt of red roses, along with a tiara of roses on her head. The rose symbolizes desire and, as with the lion, her human consciousness—her pure intention, symbolized by her white dress—shows that her desires do not control her. If we compare this simple ring of leaves and flowers on her head to the Empress's "Queen of Heaven" star crown or the High Priestess's lunar headdress, we see that Strength belongs to the earth and is grounded in nature. We might think of this card as a symbol of the environmentalist movement, helping to direct nature rather than conquering it. Despite the natural setting (no other Major card appears quite so much in nature), the yellow sky implies that mind is involved, and self-awareness, for in Western color symbolism yellow represents "mentation."

Above her head we see the same infinity sign we encountered above the Magician. Just as the Magician began the first line, Strength begins the second. True strength, in harmony with our inner nature, flows from who we are and never runs out.

So...what does Strength mean to *you*?

. . . . . .

DIVINATORY MEANINGS:

Confidence, gentle strength, openness. Overcoming destructive impulses. The ability to do something difficult with grace and courage. A person who loves animals.

REVERSED:

Weakness, doubt, possibly destructive desires that are hard to contain. Just as we might ask a querent "What does Strength mean to you?" so we can ask "What does it mean to be weak?" Reversed Strength can mean knowing your limits.

A READING FOR
Strength

1　2

3　4

5　6

1. How am I strong?

2. How am I weak?

3. When do I need to be strong?

4. When do I need to be weak?

5. What strengthens me?

6. What weakens me?

THE HERMIT.

There are some cards that people who don't know Tarot well would rather not see in a reading: Death, probably the Devil, and some of the Swords cards. In fact, each of these has valuable meanings beyond their dire titles or images, but they can unnerve people. Usually we don't think of the Hermit this way, but if you ask the cards "Will I meet my soul mate anytime soon?" and the Hermit comes up, chances are you won't be happy to see this cloaked figure all alone on a mountaintop. But perhaps you should take a second look, for it may hint that you don't really want to search for a partner right now. Maybe you want to get to know yourself better or just learn to enjoy being alone.

With little detail, the card appears quite simple, yet it contains a treasure-trove of ideas and symbols. Let's start with the Hermit himself. Carl Jung, in his theory of images found all over the world, identified a number of figures as archetypes, some in a kind of opposition to each other. One such pair is the Wise Old Man and the Eternal Child, or the Hermit and the Fool. Both stand on mountaintops, but where the Fool appears ready to leap off, the Hermit—who has climbed a higher peak—seems content to remain where he is.

He holds up a lantern, the light of wisdom, to guide the way to those who might come after him. Like the Hierophant, he is a teacher, but where the Hierophant imparts laws, the outer teachings of cultural tradition, the Hermit holds out the light of inner truth. He has no interest in disciples but will guide those who seek him out.

Inside the lantern we see a six-pointed star. Famous as a cultural symbol of Judaism, its formation from two triangles, one pointing up, the other down, originally meant the union of the two most basic principles, Fire and Water. The upward triangle represents potent, masculine Fire, while a downward triangle has symbolized the life-giving womb Water since the early Stone Age. So maybe the Hermit can end up lighting the way to love and relationship after all, for the six-pointed triangle suggests card 6, the Lovers. And, of course, the Hermit's 9 and the Lovers' 6 are mirrors of each other.

In the Major Arcana's three-level structure, the male Hermit comes below the High Priestess, while feminine Strength comes below the Magician. The seeming opposites set up at the beginning have begun to shift, even change places. We will see how the Tower, the card below the Hermit, reverses the polarity altogether.

We can see the Hermit in two ways: as ourselves or as a teacher/guide. As ourselves, the card indicates a willingness (or a need) to be on our own, to pursue our own way, and perhaps to hold up a light to our true selves. But it also may represent someone else in our lives—a teacher, a counselor, a role model, or a wise friend; someone who can light the way.

· · · · · · ·

DIVINATORY MEANINGS:

Being alone, discovering truths about yourself, a
time to look inward. Maturity, especially as an
alternative to the Fool or the adventurous knights.
Possibly a spiritual guide of some kind—a counselor,
role model, or personal teacher. Esoteric wisdom.

REVERSED:

A time to be with people, to involve yourself in society,
especially after a period of isolation. Possibly immaturity.

A READING FOR
The Hermit

1   2

5

3   4

1. What do I need to do on my own?

2. What or who is my teacher?

3. Where will I find my light?

4. What will it reveal?

5. What question does the Hermit want me to ask?

WHEEL of FORTUNE.

luck, fate, karma

The Wheel of Fortune is probably the least realistic of Smith's drawings. We see no landscape (as in Strength), no fully developed people (as in the Hermit). Instead, we find a wheel of mysterious symbols with Egyptian figures riding on it, plus an angel and three winged beasts reading books in the corners.

Most people from the Tarot's early days would recognize the four figures as the four evangelists of the gospels, Matthew, Mark, Luke, and John. But why these particular creatures? We can trace them back through several layers, including Ezekiel's vision of the heavenly chariot where he sees the same four, but ultimately they symbolize the four fixed signs of the zodiac: the angel for Aquarius, the eagle for Scorpio, the lion for Leo, and the bull for Taurus. These signs represent the seasons and thus the wheel of the year as it goes round and round. The figures also stand for the four elements of the Minor Arcana— lion / Fire, eagle / Water, angel / Air, and bull / Earth.

The thing is, these figures do not really belong on this card. You won't see them on older versions of trump 10. Waite and Smith actually imported them from the World card, where they appear more realistically, just as the fully painted world dancer, in her simple wreath, replaces the mysterious wheel full of symbols.

We have been looking at the Major Arcana as the Fool plus three rows of seven. Another approach still sets the Fool aside but then looks at two groups of ten, with Justice as a kind of linchpin between them. Card 10, the Wheel, ends the first half, and 21, the World, the second.

1 2 3 4 5 6 7 8 9 **10**

11

12 13 14 15 16 17 18 19 20 **21**

Thus, the Wheel takes us halfway, with a wisdom hidden in complex symbols, while in the World we see everything clearly.

Some see the Wheel as a promise of reincarnation. The snake on the left, a representation of the Egyptian god Seth, whom the Greeks called Typhon, symbolizes the destruction of death. On the right we see the Egyptian god Anubis, who guides dead souls to new life. At the top, the Sphinx holds the sword of truth, so we know that all our deaths and rebirths, all the ups and downs of daily life, flow from inner laws. Our lives may seem arbitrary, but they are not.

And all the symbols on the Wheel itself? The signs on the compass points signify the substances needed for alchemical transformation—mercury (north), sulfur (east), water (south), and salt (west). On the rim we find letters, English at the basic points, Hebrew in the quarter points. Starting at northeast and moving clockwise, the Hebrew spells out the famous Tetragrammaton, the most powerful name of God, which many see as a formula of creation. As well as appearing on the robe of Temperance, the letters symbolize the four suits of the Minor Arcana and the four court cards.

The four English letters can be read in different orders to form ROTA (Latin for "wheel"), TARO (Tarot), ORAT (Latin for "speaks"), TORA (Hebrew law), or ATOR (Egyptian goddess of love). The Wheel of Tarot speaks the Law of Love.

With all this symbolism, what can it mean in ordinary readings? For one thing, there is the idea of mystery, something we cannot see clearly, an unexpected turn of fate. Remember as well that carnivals often display a gambling device called a Wheel of Fortune (not to mention the TV show). Thus, it can mean taking a risk—spinning the wheel.

. . . . . .

DIVINATORY MEANINGS:

Fate, karma, but also luck. Traditionally it represents a turn for the better and so is a welcome card for someone in tough times. Things hidden that will be revealed in time. Taking a risk (especially with the Fool).

REVERSED:

A change we cannot predict or control, but possibly of less consequence than we thought. Possibly looking behind events for meaning. Another possibility: a gambling problem.

A READING FOR
The Wheel of Fortune

1

6   2

7

5   3

4

1. What turns the Wheel?

2. What outer change will come?

3. What inner change is possible?

4. What new situation will I face?

5. What rises?

6. What falls?

7. What is at the center?

KEYWORDS:
truth, self-honesty, a just outcome

In the Rider deck, Justice stands at the midpoint of the Major Arcana, with ten cards before it and ten after. The balanced scales suggest that at this halfway mark we need both to put our lives in order and begin to bring together what had seemed a duality of opposites.

Let's look a little at how that works symbolically. The Fool, zero, carries everything within, but nothing is realized. All this potential splits into two figures: the male Magician for light, consciousness, and action, and the female High Priestess for darkness, the unconscious, and stillness. We also see polar opposites with Adam and Eve in the Lovers or the black and white sphinxes of the Chariot.

Ultimately, the World will bring everything together. But look at Justice. If we do away with the Roman numerals the number becomes 11, the Magician's 1 done twice to echo the High Priestess's pillars. And, of course, 1+1=2, the number of the Priestess. The figure of Justice, a severe, androgynous woman, sits between two pillars with a curtain behind her, like the High Priestess, but her gesture of one arm up (the sword) and one down (the scales) suggests the Magician, as does the red robe and the way one foot sticks out as if she's about to stand.

So what is justice, and why is it so important? One of the cardinal virtues (along with Strength and Temperance, and Prudence, which is missing—fascinating omission), it represents the ability to look into our lives, honestly and fairly, and in so doing free ourselves from the past, with all its childhood conditioning, the influence of family and society, and even more, all the guilt and fear and resentment built up over time.

Most of us have seen the image of Justice on courthouses. There the scales often tilt, for the courts must decide who wins and who loses. And courthouse Justice wears a blindfold for impartiality. Tarot Justice, however, wears no blindfold and seems to stare straight at us, as if challenging us to look honestly at our lives.

The sword points straight up for truth. In all the cards, only three cards point upright—Justice, the Ace of Swords, and the Queen of Swords.

People often ask, if the Tarot can predict events, what of free will? First of all, the cards do not show hard predictions but possibilities. More deeply, we always have free will, but we often don't use it. This is because we act based on unconscious needs. Justice challenges us to really become conscious of who we are so we can make genuinely free choices.

But what of actual court cases? The Tarot, even in its deepest cards, never abandons the everyday. If you ask about a legal issue and Justice comes up, there is likely to be a just outcome. Of course, this does not guarantee the outcome you desire.

· · · · · ·

DIVINATORY MEANINGS:

*Self-examination, balancing different issues in your life,
honesty. A moral choice. A just outcome in a legal case.*

REVERSED:

*Unwillingness to look honestly at yourself or your
part in some issue. Possibly an unjust or unfair
situation. Unjust outcome in a legal case.*

A READING FOR
Justice (for conflict situations)

7

1   4

2 3   5 6

(IN THE FORM OF SCALES)

1. What is outer justice?

2. What is the wisdom of pursuing it?

3. What action is best?

4. What is inner justice?

5. What part do I play?

6. How will justice come about?

7. What is the link between inner and outer justice?

THE HANGED MAN.

KEYWORDS:
attachment, suspension, unconventionality

From the almost crowded symbolism of the Wheel to the balanced scales of Justice to the Hanged Man, we come to one of the Tarot's most enigmatic pictures. The first time people leaf through the deck, they may turn this card around, as if it got stuck in the box upside down. There are even some old decks where the printer made this mistake and placed the number in such a way that the figure has to be seen right-side up. But his upside-downness is essential, for he has taken the truth of Justice and turned his life around.

It may be that part of the card's basic meaning is to be mis-understood. After all, if you're upside down from everyone else, people are likely to think you're just *wrong*. But look at the picture, his relaxed posture, his radiant face. Does he seem to care about society's opinions of him?

Many see this card in a negative way. *Hung up. Stuck. Painful sacrifice.* In Italy people used to hang traitors upside down by their feet, and thus some decks show the body contorted and the face in pain, with the title the Traitor. But this is not what *this* picture shows. The Hanged Man is the only figure whose face shines with golden light; not even the angels appear so transfigured. He has attached himself to the tree of his deep-est spiritual values, and it no longer matters if people approve or disapprove of him.

In the number 12, 1, the Magician, and 2, the High Priest-ess come together; 12 is also 21 backwards, and if we put the World alongside the Hanged Man (or maybe the World above and the Hanged Man below), we will see they are almost the same posture. It's as if halfway through the Major Arcana we can glimpse the wonders of the end of the journey—but only if we turn ourselves upside down, that is, the opposite of our previous way of seeing life.

The crosslike posture points to the cards around it. The horizontal leg reminds us that it comes poised between Justice and Death, the place where we have accepted the truth of who we are and the place where we surrender to change. If we see the Major Arcana as triads, vertical rows, then the extended leg points to the Hierophant above and the head to the radiant Sun below. He plants his foot in tradition and his head in the bright light of revelation. And, of course, he can only do this by being upside down—different from the people around him.

Does this mean we should ignore those people who state firmly that the Hanged Man means suffering or painful sacrifice? Well, the card itself reminds us that you do not have to accept anyone else's authority (including mine). But we certainly can see a truth to this view. It all depends on how we "do" Justice. That is, if we truly can balance the scales and accept ourselves, then the Hanged Man is a joyous attachment to deep values and spiritual revelation. But if we resist the truth of Justice, then the Hanged Man may become some painful issue—a life situation or just a memory or fear—from which we cannot untie ourselves.

· · · · · ·

DIVINATORY MEANINGS:

Attachment to deep values. Seeing things differently
than those around you. Joy, even revelation.
Alternatively, being stuck, or a sacrifice.

REVERSED:

Overly influenced by social expectations or others'
opinions and beliefs about you. Possibly untying yourself
from a situation and being ready to move on.

A READING FOR
The Hanged Man

1

2

3 4

5

1. How am I different from the people around me?

2. What are my deep values?

3. What brings me pain?

4. What brings me joy?

5. What can I discover?

DEATH.

change, something that needs to end

Almost the first thing a Tarot reader has to learn is to not fear the Death card. To put it another way: if Death shows up in a reading, do not expect that someone has to die, and certainly do not think that the card will somehow magically cause someone to die. The Tarot neither compels behavior nor shapes reality. There are seventy-eight cards in a Tarot deck. If the only function of one of them was to predict death, it would be taking up space without being of much use.

Then what *does* card 13 mean? There are many things that can die besides the body—old habits, lifestyles, dead-end jobs, a lifeless relationship that may already feel dead. Maybe something has to die for a person to come back to life. The Tarot carries an inbuilt optimism, and the death of something in our lives does not have to leave us as a corpse. A powerful angel follows the Death card; Temperance can symbolize what is liberated when we allow what is old and worn out to end. Angels, in fact, surround Death. The card appears in the sixth position of the second row. Above it, an angel spreads his wings above the Lovers, while below, another angel blows his horn for the dead to rise from their coffins. Love, Death, and Resurrection. And notice that the people above and below Death, the Lovers and Judgement, are naked, completely open to blessings and joy.

Older versions of Death showed a cloaked skeleton with a scythe "harvesting" hands and feet and crowned heads. The lesson was that it doesn't matter who you are or how important and powerful; Death takes all of us. The Rider version of Death is more complicated and more subtle. The skeleton has become even more imposing in black armor, on a stately white horse with fiery eyes. The white rose banner symbolizes Death's power and purity.

The card abounds with symbols. Look all the way to the left. Do you see the Egyptian boat in the river? In the famous Book of the Dead, the Egyptians described death as a transition from one state to another. The four people along the bottom of the card represent different ways of responding to the letting go demanded by Death. A dead king lies under the horse, as if trampled. He signifies whatever resists change—the rigid ego that cannot give up control. A bishop stands before the horse, hands up in a gesture of prayer. Standing stiffly, as if his elaborate robe holds him up, he symbolizes teachings and traditions that allow people to face Death without fear. There are many such teachings; for example, the "other" Book of the Dead, from Tibet (not the actual title for either one). What they seem to have in common is the importance of not getting stuck in fear of Death but instead traveling through the experience to a new life on the other side.

At the bishop's feet we see a child and a maiden, both with flowers in their hair. The maiden looks away, as if she has become just self-aware enough to be scared. The child, on the other hand, symbolizes innocence and freedom from fear. He faces Death with a bouquet of fresh flowers.

. . . . . .

DIVINATORY MEANINGS:

The end of something. The need to release something without fear or regret; usually this will lead to new possibilities. When physical death is actually an issue, the card calls on us to look at it honestly.

REVERSED:

Fear of change. Rigidity. Stagnation. Sometimes (when the reading concerns sickness or old age) fear of physical death, though not a statement that the person will soon die.

A READING FOR
Death, based on the White Rose
(designed by Paula C. Scardamalia)

¹/ 6   3

4   5

2

1. What has already died?

2. What killed it?

3. What needs to die?

4. What will release it?

5. What is buried?

6 (placed on top of card 1). What can be born?

calm, balance, sobriety

The word *temperance* used to mean to abstain from alcohol. Even though the picture looks a little like the angel is mixing a cocktail, it indicates calmness, responsibility, and, yes, abstinence. But it is also far more, for we see an angel, after all, and it follows Death. Though we think of him as an archangel, he also symbolizes what I call our "angelic selves," the qualities we discover in ourselves when we pass successfully through the challenges of surrender and release.

Notice that what the angel is doing is actually impossible, since water will not pour at an angle. One meaning of this card is to calmly do something you used to think was beyond your capabilities. The angel appears peaceful, focused, even unemotional, yet the wings beat so powerfully the picture cannot contain them.

Temperance is the second of the three "victories," cards 7, 14, and 21—the Chariot, Temperance, and the World. This is a victory over fear, guilt, ignorance, and whatever holds us back from the discovery of the divine angel within each of us. One example of this victory would be the alcoholic who stops drinking. But that is only one example, playing on the word.

In the Middle Ages, people believed that the body contained various "tempers" that controlled both health and behavior. We became sick or acted badly when one of these dominated and the body became unbalanced. This is probably the origin of the expression "lose your temper." Temperance means to keep your energies and actions in balance and harmony. Thus, as well as calm and moderation, Temperance can mean overall good health—and in certain situations it can mean to *not* lose your temper.

The symbolism of the picture carries us beyond the everyday psychological meanings. I see the angel as Michael, whose name means the one "who is like God." If you look carefully at the folds of the robe, above the square, you will find the Hebrew letters we saw on the Wheel of Fortune, yod-heh-vav-heh. In Christian myth, Michael led God's side in the war against Lucifer. It was Michael who cast Lucifer into the dark abyss to become Satan. This is one reason why the Devil comes after Temperance. Temperance represents not just self-control but a genuine victory over our own temptations, such as addictions, pride, or self-hate.

He stands with one foot on a rock, the other in water, another example of blended energy, for the water symbolizes the emotions while the rock represents grounding ourselves in the "real world" beyond ourselves. On his head he wears a circle with a dot in it, the astrological symbol of the sun. We also see the sun, which had just risen in Death, now shining above the mountains: new life, but also higher consciousness.

A road leads from the water to the mountains. We might think of this road as the path of calm, tempered behavior. The flowers to the right are irises. In Greek myth, Iris officiated in oaths taken by the gods. Thus, Temperance can mean a serious or solemn oath, or a commitment to a new life.

. . . . . .

DIVINATORY MEANINGS:

Calm, moderation, a sense of inner balance.
Commitment, especially to a new life. Creative problem-
solving by combining different ideas or energies.

REVERSED:

Intemperate. Losing control. Excessive behavior or going
to extremes; this is not always a bad thing. Possibly,
with other cards, giving way to an addiction.

A READING FOR
Temperance

1   2

3

4

5   6

Can be used for people facing a difficult choice or situations with extreme contradictions.

1. Current situation

2. Alternative

3. Possible middle way

4. Needed approach

5. How to let energy flow

6. What commitment is needed

THE DEVIL.

KEYWORDS:
obsessions, bad relationships, low desires or beliefs
(but also sexual life energy)

There is a strange idea about the Tarot that we sometimes encounter: that Satan himself literally invented Tarot and gave it to humanity as a way to lure people into sin. In fact, the Tarot is, above all else, a spiritual document, and while the Devil card may highlight our weaknesses, or the darkness within us, the most important symbol is the chains that seemingly hold the two people. If you look at the loops, you'll see they're loose enough for the people to take them off and walk away. We are always free to make our own choices. No matter how bad a situation may appear, no matter how low we may believe we have gone, we can change things.

The Devil's number is 15, and 1+5=6, the Lovers. Put the two cards together and you will see that the Devil appears as a kind of dark parody of the Lovers. The fruit and leaves of the trees behind Adam and Eve have become the tails of the people turned into semi-demons by their allegiance to the Devil. Thus, the card can mean bad relationships, sometimes abusive or obsessive.

And yet, if we look at the picture, the people do not appear unhappy; their bodies are at ease, a slight smile is upon their faces. Some Tarot readers rebel against what they consider a sexually repressive society and see the Devil as a card of sexuality, or wild times. One woman I read for said it was her favorite card, because it meant party time. The image of people held by chains may hint at bondage or other sexual games that can appear disturbing but are actually harmless. One source for the image is the Greek god Pan, who was, among other things, the god of orgies!

Waite and Smith's image actually derives from Baphomet, a demon supposedly worshiped by the Knights Templar. Some people believe that the Templars found and protected the Holy Grail, whose image appears as the Ace of Cups.

The Devil's number, 15, consists of 1, the Magician, and 5, the Hierophant. Like the Hierophant, the Devil rules over two disciples. He also raises his hand in a parody of the Hierophant's blessings, but his open hand, compared to the Hierophant's two fingers up and two down, implies that the material world is all that exists. No above and below, no greater truth, just what you can see and touch in front of you. Notice that where the Magician raises his crystal wand, as if toward heaven, the Devil points his fiery torch down at the ground.

Like the Magician, the Devil begins a line of seven cards, the final group that ends with the World. Why does it come at this late point? Maybe we need to find our angelic selves in Temperance before we take on the challenge of the last line, which is nothing less than the liberation of whatever spiritual light is trapped in darkness. Lay out the seven cards and look at the movement of light. Total darkness in the Devil, lightning in the Tower, then Starlight, Moonlight, Sunlight, and greater and greater light until we come to what I call the Light of the Spirit in Judgement and the Light of the Self in the World.

· · · · · ·

DIVINATORY MEANINGS:

Oppression, addictive behavior, bad relationships;
whatever chains us. Illusions, mistakes, sometimes lies.
More lightly, wild times, rebellion, sexual adventures.

REVERSED:

Steps toward liberation. Recognizing free choice.
Seeing through illusions. Becoming serious and
responsible, especially in a relationship.

A READING FOR
The Devil

1   3

4   5

2

(IN THE SHAPE OF THE

INVERSE PENTAGRAM)

1. What illusory chains hold me?

2. How can I see through the illusion?

3. How do I free myself?

4. What will I discover?

5. What is the first step?

THE TOWER.

upheaval, release, revelation

Tarot readings usually concern personal issues, though some questions may reach out beyond the querent. Every now and then, however, the world seems to intrude on personal readings. After September 11, 2001, Tarot readers as far from New York as Australia reported that for some two weeks before the terrorist attack on the twin towers, the Tower card appeared in every reading they did, no matter the subject.

So does the Tower mean calamity, even actual death? The simple answer is no. Such a response to world events is very rare. It does, however, indicate an upheaval or sudden turn-around, often necessary to release people from a difficult situation. The Tarot is essentially optimistic but not always gentle. If some kind of pressure builds up, we may need for it to explode around us to free us. After the Tower comes the calm and beautiful Star.

An interesting contemporary interpretation sees the Tower as orgasm (especially male, from the imagery), and thus the power of sex in general to change our lives. If the Devil might represent an illicit affair, the Tower could signify its discovery.

We can look at the card more positively. The lightning overthrows some entrenched situation that had become as rigid as a stone tower without a door. Energy is released, and everything changes. We've looked at various cards that show duality, the seemingly fixed opposites of life, symbolized as a man, or a light figure, on the right, and a woman, or dark figure, on the left. We can think of the Lovers, the Devil, and the Chariot's two sphinxes. The Tower's 16 reduces to 7, the Chariot, but it also contains the number 6, the Lovers. In the Tower the polarity becomes reversed: the man on the left, the woman on the right.

Some people see the Tower as Babel, when humans tried to build a tower to Heaven, only to have God strike it with lightning and break up their unified speech into many languages. This emphasizes the Tower's destructive side. But we also might think of Pentecost, in which the Holy Spirit enters people like lightning and they "speak in tongues," wild sounds that transcend ordinary human language. Shamans all over the world do the same thing when they go into a trance state. This is the Tower as "divine speech," or revelation.

The drops of fire on either side of the Tower take the form of the Hebrew letter yod ('), the first letter of the mystical name found on the Wheel and on Temperance. Yod represents the element Fire, for inspiration and new beginnings. We see ten on the right and twelve on the left—ten for our ten fingers (and thus the practical world below), and twelve for the zodiac (and so the spiritual world above). Together they form twenty-two, the number of cards in the Major Arcana.

What does all this symbolism mean for our readings? The Tower does not only mean destruction, it also can mean release of energy or some powerful revelation that changes everything. The change is usually positive, even if it feels painful in the moment. The lightning topples the crown from the Tower. Babies usually emerge from their mothers upside down, and we call the moment when they leave the narrow birth canal and enter the wide world "crowning."

. . . .

DIVINATORY MEANINGS:

An explosive situation, upheaval. Sometimes extreme conditions, possibly even violence. Revelation, whether spiritual or a shocking discovery. Liberation. The sudden end of a long-standing problem.

REVERSED:

Waite says "the same in a lesser degree." Situations are not as extreme, or people hold in their reactions. But there may not be the sense of liberation and release.

A READING FOR
The Tower

1

3   5   4

2

1. What structures my life?

2. How has it supported me?

3. How has it confined me?

4. What will break it apart?

5. What will emerge?

THE STAR.

KEYWORDS:
hope, optimism, peace

In the sequence of the Major Arcana, the most difficult section—the Fool's Crisis, we might call it—begins with Death and reaches its culmination in the explosiveness of the Tower. The Star shows us that we have come through—we have cast off the Devil's chains and found hope and openness. The Star resembles Temperance, the card between Death and the Devil, with some important differences. There we saw a powerful angel with divine symbols hidden in his robe. Here we see only a nude woman. There are five "naked" cards in the Rider

Major Arcana (six, if you count the World), and all but the Lovers appear in the final group of seven cards. These cards take us beyond symbolic ideas to direct experience of powerful change.

Both Temperance and the Star show one foot on land and one in water—or *on* water in the Star's case, for her foot does not seem to penetrate the ripples of the pond. What does this almost miraculous posture mean? If we see the water as the unconscious, the pool behind the High Priestess's curtain, then we can stir it up and allow it to ripple but never truly penetrate it. In the next card, the Moon, we will see a creature half emerge from a similar pool.

Temperance pours water miraculously at an angle, careful not to spill a drop. The Star maiden pours water from two natural gourds, with nothing held back. This gesture links the card to Persephone, the Greek goddess of death and rebirth whose pomegranates we saw on the High Priestess's curtain. At the end of Persephone's Mysteries, a ritual held at the end of summer, the celebrants, led by the Hierophant, poured water from two vessels into cracks in the earth, calling out "Hye! Kye!" ("Rain! Conceive!") to rejuvenate the ground after summer's drought. Persephone's mother, Demeter, appears as the Empress, and the third triad runs Empress, Wheel of Fortune, Star. When both the Empress and the Star appear in a reading, they may symbolize a strong mother-daughter relationship.

Various people have suggested what actual star the card might indicate. (Remember, we have no record of what the deck's original designers had in mind.) Some have said Polaris, the compass star that never deviates from its position over the North Pole, so that people can use it to navigate. And the eight- pointed Star resembles a compass, as does the eight-spoked Wheel of Fortune above it.

For myself, I see the Star as the planet Venus, called the Morning Star, the third brightest object in the sky after the sun and moon, and thus part of the natural progression of Star-light, Moonlight, and Sunlight. As the goddess of love, Venus is (like Demeter) the Empress, who bears Venus's planetary symbol on her shield. But Venus is also the Devil, whom the Christians name Lucifer Morningstar. Venus disappears from the sky for part of the year, so maybe the Devil is love trapped in darkness, and the Star shows us Venus's return, love reborn.

We can see a modern meaning in the very title of this card. Be a star. Shine. Don't hide who you are, don't let the Devil chain you with fears of people's disapproval or scorn. Pour out your waters and discover your natural grace and beauty.

· · · · · ·

DIVINATORY MEANINGS:

Hope, openness, calm, especially after a crisis or an explosion of some sort. Healing and regeneration. Be a star. Let others see the real you. Sensuality, physical confidence.

REVERSED:

Doubt, pessimism, possibly a false hope. Shyness, sometimes a genuine need to hide something about yourself, at least in some particular situation.

A READING FOR
The Star

Take out the Star card, look at it for a while, then set it on the table. Mix the rest of the deck and turn over one to three cards for each of the following themes:

A. Hope

B. Guidance

C. Peace

D. Healing

THE MOON.

KEYWORDS:
instinct, intuition, lunacy, mystery

Except perhaps for the Wheel of Fortune, with its jackal-headed god, the Moon is the only Major Arcana card with animals instead of people. Instead of Adam and Eve in the Lovers, or the two disciples in the Hierophant, we see a dog and a wolf, and in the place of the dominant third figure above the two is the Moon itself. We also see a figure below, a crayfish half-emerged from the pool, as if the Star stirred up the deep waters and now something very primitive struggles to come to the surface. Right in the center of the Major Arcana's final line of seven, the Moon forms the Fool's last great test. We might imagine a fairy tale in which a magic spell transforms a beautiful boy into a wolf, with his loyal dog still beside him. And fairy tales, myths, stories, and even our dreams are said to come through the moon's strange half-light.

The Fool's fairy tale comes to a good end, for in the next card, the Sun, we see a joyous child riding a horse in what Waite calls "perfect conformity" of our divine consciousness and animal nature.

But what of the crayfish? Waite calls it that which lies "lower than the savage beast." It symbolizes stirrings from the most primitive parts of our brain, the fears and instincts that we cannot even name. The crayfish only half emerges and will fall back again (or so the traditional interpretation tells us). If we fight or deny the wild sides of ourselves, we may distort who we are. If we accept ourselves completely, like the naked Star maiden, we can find peace with the strangeness of our most primitive instincts.

Does the moon really cause such powerful reactions? Does Luna inspire lunacy? Police and hospital workers will generally insist that the three days of the full moon bring trouble and strangeness. People who have examined police blotters and hospital records say it's not actually true, but people *believe* it is.

The moon does not actually shine by itself but reflects the sun, so that occultists often describe it as a half-truth. In recent years, Tarotists, especially women, have challenged such negativity. The moon's rotation matches women's menstrual cycles (the strongest example of "as above, so below"), and people have reclaimed the ancient link between the moon's phases of waxing, full, and waning and the Triple Goddess of Maiden, Mother, and Crone.

The Tarot Moon no longer means primarily animal instincts and lunacy. We think of it more as intuition, psychic awareness, and a sense of the mysteries of existence.

The Moon also signifies dreams, myths, and fantasies—not the clear, bright truths of the Sun but the wondrous waters of imagination. This is one reason why Tarot readers sometimes have trouble distinguishing genuine psychic flashes from imagined stories: they both come from the same place. The Moon represents a strange territory of wildness and mystery, the Fool's final test between the relaxed Star and the confident Sun. But its half-light also hides treasures of the mind. "The myth is the penultimate truth" wrote the philosopher Ananda Coomaraswamy. For those of us who love the imagination, that is more than good enough.

. . . . . .

DIVINATORY MEANINGS:

Mystery, deep instincts, imagination. Strange and
possibly disturbing energy. Psychic abilities. In extreme
situations, madness. Strong dreams. Stories, creativity.
Possibly alignment with the cycles of nature.

REVERSED:

Something waning, on the way out. Not knowing how
to handle disturbing emotions. Possibly mood swings or
depression. Alternatively, if the Moon reversed appears with
the Sun or other solar cards (such as the Ace of Wands),
a lunar time is ending and life will become simpler.

A READING FOR
The Moon

1   2

3   4

5

1. What phase of the moon am I in—
   waxing, full, or waning?

2. What benefits does it bring me?

3. How does it challenge me?

4. How can I meet the challenge?

5. What will come next?

THE SUN .

clarity, happiness, freedom

At night, under the moon, everything appears strange, half visible, half in darkness. But when the sun comes out, the way becomes clear. What might have seemed like a malevolent spirit becomes revealed as just a tree. Thus, the Sun card means clarity and the rational mind, with its ability to see and understand the truth. As well as a clear contrast with the Moon, the Sun also completes the liberation of light trapped in the Devil's darkness. In the Kabbalistic interpretation of Tarot, each Major Arcana card is linked to a Hebrew letter.

The letter for the Sun card, resh, means "head," in particular the cerebral cortex, the part of us that can think and reason.

In ancient Greece, the god Apollo, ruler of the sun, brought civilization to struggling humanity. His sister, Artemis, ruled the wild places of nature, the forests and mountains. But Apollo is not simply rationality, for he also ruled music, poetry (the nine Muses lived on his favorite mountain, Parnassus), and, most significantly for us, the power of prophecy. At the greatest oracle center of the ancient world, Delphi, a woman known as the Pythia would go into trance and become the direct voice of Apollo. Thus the Sun card subtly can refer to the power of the seer to reveal truths.

The Sun forms one of the Rider deck's traditional departures from traditional Tarot design. In the Tarot of Marseille, Waite and Smith's primary model, the Sun shows two people, usually children, sometimes two boys but more often a boy and a girl, together in a walled garden. After all the images of opposites, from the poles of the High Priestess all the way to the dog and the wolf of the Moon, two come together in harmony. In the following card, Judgement, a child stands between a man and a woman; duality overcome, a new self arises. Then why change the Sun card to show a single child?

The movement of the figure away from the wall gives a sense of freedom, while the child's bright countenance shows us innocence and joy. The Fool has returned to childlike simplicity. Notice that the Sun child wears the same red feather that the Fool carried in his hat, while the banner he waves resembles the sash wound around the World dancer. Even more than the Fool and his dog, the child on the horse symbolizes what Waite calls the "perfect conformity" of spiritual openness and animal nature.

Waite apparently designed his Sun card from a Belgian Tarot deck called Bacchus (Bacchus, the god of wine, replaces the Pope/Hierophant!). That deck, however, showed a grown man, a warrior it seems, riding across the card and waving a banner of victory. Instead of triumph, the child in the Rider image symbolizes openness to transformation and spiritual light. A lifelong Christian, Waite may have been thinking of the famous statement by Jesus, "Except ye be converted and become as little children, ye shall not enter into the Kingdom of Heaven."

The Sun gives off eleven straight rays and ten undulating ones. Together they make twenty-one, the number of the World card. But what of the twenty-second card, the Fool? Look at the squiggly black line to the right of the Roman numerals. Does it represent a simple printer's error or the Fool's hidden presence as a twenty-second ray?

・ ・ ・ ・ ・ ・ ・

DIVINATORY MEANINGS:

Openness, joy, simplicity. Clear thinking. The rational mind. Good health, happiness, brightness.

REVERSED:

As with the Tower, Waite says "the same in a lesser degree." It's as if the Sun shines so brightly it cannot lose its positive nature, even when reversed, but maybe some clouds obscure the light. Happiness may mix with sadness, or an issue become less clear.

A READING FOR
The Sun

```
                    1
        4     5     2
              3
```

1. What is clear about an issue or a situation?

2. What is clouded over?

3. What helps me see clearly?

4. What confuses me?

5. How can I simplify this issue or situation?

JUDGEMENT.

KEYWORDS:
great change, restored relationship,
family or group happiness

The source for this image goes back to Medieval and Renaissance paintings of the biblical Last Judgement (I use the British spelling because that's how it appears on the card). The angel Gabriel blows his horn and the dead rise up, some taken to Heaven but the majority sent down to the flames and pitchforks of Hell. Because of these associations, many people, especially those with too-vivid memories of Sunday school or scary sermons, find the card of Judgement and the very name disturbing. They fear that someone, maybe even themselves, will judge them. Somehow they never expect a positive outcome, maybe because their Sunday school teachers told them that only the very few, the saintly, go to Heaven. And how many of us think of ourselves as saintly?

But look at the picture. Notice the joy and wonder in the six people rising from what appear to be open coffins. No one is being judged. No one is being sent anywhere. Instead, we see a great rising up, symbolic of a change in consciousness, one that may have been building for a long time but seems to happen all of a sudden.

Paul Foster Case criticized Waite's design for this card. The three people in front, he wrote, were sufficient for the symbolism, so why add the extra family in the back? To me, they signify the way one person's transformation affects everyone around her.

But what is that "sufficient" symbolism? Throughout the Major Arcana we have seen images of duality, including, at the top of the sixth triad, the Lovers card, with the man on the right and the woman on the left. Below 6 comes 13, Death, and below that 20, Judgement. Love, death, and resurrection. And in that bottom card the polarity becomes reversed, with the man on the left and the woman on the right, as if everything has changed. Once again, however, the woman becomes the primary link to Above. In the Lovers, it was Eve who looked up at the angel Raphael. Here the woman opens her arms to receive Gabriel's trumpet blast of renewal.

But now something new has appeared. A child stands with outspread arms, like the Sun child in the previous card. We don't see its face—it signifies something completely new, beyond all previous experience. We cannot see if the child is male or female. The new self transcends polarity.

Waite makes clear that the horn does not signify an apocalyptic end of the world but a spiritual transformation. "What is that within us," he writes, "that sounds a trumpet and all that is low in our nature rises in response?" The card's number, 20, reduces to 2, and just as we saw the waters of the unconscious behind the High Priestess's curtain, so here the coffins of our old selves open on the waves of the sea.

When this wonderful card appears in a reading, it may tell us that a great change is already happening. In the querent's life something has sounded the trumpet, and everything becomes different. The challenge now is to recognize and believe in this powerful new beginning.

. . . . . .

DIVINATORY MEANINGS:

A fresh start. Renewal, especially of a relationship, whether romantic or family, that had seemed dead. Outer realization of a great change that has already happened internally. Family or group celebration.

REVERSED:

Fear or doubt that holds a person back from accepting change or opportunity. The trumpet still sounds, but we don't trust it.

A READING FOR
Judgement

1

2   3

4   5

1. What calls me to rise up and become something new?

2. What can I become?

3. How will my life change?

4. How will my change affect others?

5. How am I called to answer?

THE WORLD.

success, fulfillment, great understanding

One of Smith's most graceful pictures, the World culminates the Major Arcana. This is the last and most triumphant of the three "victories," cards 7, the Chariot; 14, Temperance; and now 21, the World. The woman in the picture dances within a wreath, traditional symbol of a great victory. The higher consciousness that was held in chains in the Devil, at the start of the line, is now fully liberated.

Where the four figures in the corners of the Wheel of Fortune appeared cartoonish, only symbolic and nothing more, here we see them realistically drawn, almost as elegant as the dancer herself. The figures represent the four fixed signs of the zodiac and, by extension, the seasons of the year—the bull for Taurus (spring), the lion for Leo (summer), the eagle for Scorpio (autumn), and the human—not an angel, as in the Wheel—for Aquarius (winter). We see only the heads, symbol of consciousness, emerging from clouds, as if from a world beyond our normal perception. In the Minor Arcana aces, hands similarly emerge from clouds to offer the objects of the suit—the wand, cup, sword, and pentacle we see lying on the table of the Magician. The cards 1 and 21, the beginning and end of the Fool's journey, become subtly united as well as linked to the four suits of the Minor Arcana.

In all the Major Arcana, only the Fool and the World show people in motion—dancing with their arms out—while all the other figures stand or sit or kneel in fixed postures. There are other connections between the Fool and the World, the beginning and the end. The World's victory wreath takes the form of the Fool's number, 0, tied on top and bottom with red sashes in the shape of the infinity sign ∞. As above, so below. With the Fool, we reminded ourselves that if you divide any number by zero, the result is always infinity.

Though a young man, the Fool appeared androgynous (as, in fact, do so many of Smith's characters), with both masculine and feminine qualities. The World dancer appears as a woman, but a long-standing tradition sees her as secretly hermaphroditic, with male as well as female organs hidden under the sash. And probably the main source for the earliest image of this card *was* masculine—paintings of Christ risen from the tomb and ascending to Heaven. Where the Fool contained all possibilities with nothing realized, the World brings every-thing to fulfillment. The Fool is innocence, the World wisdom, but both show us a complete person.

The number 21 contains 2, the High Priestess, and 1, the Magician. The dancer holds two of the Magician's double-ended wands, one on each side, like the pillars of the High Priestess. She dances forward, to the future, while looking over her shoulder toward the past.

What is most remarkable about this picture is that all these symbols and ideas come to us in such a graceful, natural form. As we look at the card, we can feel the deep truths in our own bodies. This is the great secret of Tarot reading: to become the cards.

· · · · · ·

DIVINATORY MEANINGS:

Success, breakthrough, a powerful understanding.
Fulfillment. Wholeness and freedom. Sometimes
indicates recognition from the outer world.

REVERSED:

Stagnation or delays rather than failure. Possibly
life or a situation becoming more structured, more
stable. Less susceptible to sudden changes.

A READING FOR
The World

1

3   5   4

2

1. Where am I coming from?

2. Where am I stepping to?

3. What do I hold for myself?

4. What do I give others?

5. What new thing awaits me?

The Minor Arcana

Where the Major Arcana shows us the great story of the Fool's Journey, the Minor brings us a kaleidoscope of experiences in four suits, each with the same structure yet colored by the suit's special quality, ten numbers, and four court cards.

Consider card games. In most games, it doesn't really matter which suit it is—a four of clubs is basically the same as a four of spades. In Tarot, however, the Four of Wands is quite different from the Four of Swords. They share what we might call "fourness," but the suit's energy changes them. Taken together, the fifty-six Minor cards give us scenes and characters from our lives.

The Minor cards actually consist of two different sets, the "pips," or numbered cards—ace through ten—and the court cards: page, knight, queen, and king. Most books look at each suit as a whole; for example, Ace of Wands through King of Wands. Lately I have found it valuable to look at them separately, for the numbers indicate events and situations, while the courts evoke people—either actual persons, such as the famous "tall dark stranger" of fortunetellers—or character traits. The qualities of each suit belong to both groups. Just as the Four of Wands combines fourness with Wands, so the Queen of Wands shows us the qualities of the queen in the confident world of fiery Wands.

The Suits

Before we look at either the number or the court cards, let's look at what they have in common: the suits. The most common way we understand the suits is by the four traditional elements of Fire, Water, Air, and Earth. This division of life goes back thousands of years and is found in many traditions, including astrology and alchemy (we made references to the elements in the astrological correspondences for the Major Arcana). In the Rider deck, Wands belong to Fire, Cups to Water, Swords to Air, and Pentacles to Earth.

Fire represents the first spark of creation, warmth, action, energy, confidence. Water expresses feelings, especially love and relationships, imagination, intuition, family. Air shows us the mind, which, like Air, we cannot see but which affects us constantly. We can experience Air gently, as in contemplation, or wildly, as in anger like a storm. Because Tarot depicts Air with a sword, the pictures tend to show scenes of conflict or sorrow. The element of Earth evokes solidness, stability. It concerns money and work—the original symbol for this suit was a coin—but also nature. The pentacle itself, a five-pointed star in a circle, has become the symbol of the earth-based religion of Wicca.

Here are the suits and elements, listed with their qualities:

WANDS:

Fire—masculine energy—action, optimism, sexual desire, adventure, forcefulness, competition.

CUPS:

Water—feminine energy—emotion, love, relationship, imagination, happiness, sadness, family.

SWORDS:

Air—mind—mental activity, conflict, heroism, grief, justice and injustice.

PENTACLES:

Earth—body—nature, work, money, possessions, security.

None of these qualities exist in isolation but combine, conflict, and move in and out of each other. The primary way we experience this is through readings, where the cards come together in endless variations and patterns.

Wands and Cups tend to be positive and optimistic, with Swords and Pentacles darker, more difficult. At the same time, Wands and Pentacles deal with action and work—things outside ourselves—while Cups and Swords deal with the intangible qualities of emotion and thought.

Of course, the pip cards are not just suits, they are also numbers: one, or ace, to ten. There are many, *many* ways in which people have looked at these numbers, individually and as a group, but rather than link them to any of the various systems, we can go right to the heart of the pictures themselves.

Some time ago, it struck me that we could take the four cards of each number—for example, the Two of Wands, the Two of Cups, the Two of Swords, and the Two of Pentacles—and just see what they have in common. This way we can see what theme, or shared energy, belongs to each number.

One of the fascinating things about this exercise is the discovery that sometimes the theme works against the element. For example, the four eights share a theme of movement. We see this clearly in the flying sticks of Wands, or the man in Cups leaving things behind to climb a hill under the moon, or even the Pentacles figure calmly chiseling one pentacle after another. But what of the tied-up woman in Swords? Well, if someone has tied you up, blindfolded you, and placed swords all around you so that you cannot move at all, doesn't that make "movement" the most important issue in your life at that moment?

What follows are my own observations; they are by no means an absolute truth. I strongly urge you to set out the cards for yourself and see what you discover.

Aces

Pure energy of the suit, a gift of the Spirit. In each card, a hand emerges from a cloud and holds out the emblem of the suit, as if we just need to reach out and take it. The aces are the simplest of the ten numbers.

Twos

Choices or the attempt to find balance. Wands have to choose between security and adventure, Cups find balance in relationship, Swords resist choice by blindfolding the mind, while Pentacles balance aspects of life in a loop shaped like infinity.

Threes

A flowering or something created from the energy of the suit. For Wands, this is rootedness; for Cups, friendship; for Swords, heartbreak; for Pentacles, masterful work.

Fours

Structure—from the simple bower of Wands (Fire does not like to be contained), to Cups' hesitation to try something new, to Swords' retreat into restfulness, to Pentacles' use of money or possessions to protect and define our lives.

Fives

Life's difficulties. While fiery Wands get energized by conflict, Cups grieve, Swords suffer a humiliating defeat, and that couple in Pentacles find themselves crippled, penniless, and walking barefoot through the snow. This disturbing theme comes from a famous Kabbalistic diagram known as the Tree of Life. The Tree actually appears as the layout of the disks on the Ten of Pentacles, but we find glimpses of it elsewhere, including the top half on the Five of Pentacles.

On the Tree, the fifth position is a place of harshness, and so the fives become the most difficult group of cards.

Sixes

Unequal relationships, but out of that may come the possibility of generosity. In each card, one person stands above and superior to a single person (Cups), a pair of people (Swords and Pentacles), or a whole group (Wands). From this position, however, they act generously to those around them. The Wands horseman shares his optimism and confidence with those who walk alongside him; the older child in the Six of Cups gives a flower to the younger; the man in Swords ferries the figures in the boat; while the Six of Pentacles shows us an image of charity.

Sevens

Action or maybe just the *contemplation* of action. The figure in Wands knows he must stay on top; the Cups person fantasizes about possibilities; the Swords character sneaks off with an armful of swords; and the Pentacles farmer looks at his garden with satisfaction or concern (depending how you read his expression).

Eights

Movement. Wands fly through the air; a man leaves cups behind; a blindfolded woman in Swords finds it hard to move at all; and an artisan develops his skill, creating one pentacle after another.

Nines

Intensity, the element at a high degree. Wands shows courage and strength; Cups, satisfaction; Swords, grief; and Pentacles, discipline that produces success.

Tens

Excess. The responsibilities of Wands bends the back; Cups celebrate family happiness; Swords suffers; and Pentacles live in splendor but possibly do not see the magic outside their material comfort.

· · · · · ·

Wands

ACE of WANDS.

ELEMENT:
fire

THEME:
pure energy of suit, a gift

A white hand emerges from a gray cloud, with a live stick held in a firm grip. The sky itself appears gray, as does the distant castle below, so that the Wand seems to offer brightness and fresh life to a dull world. Curiously, the sky appears gray in the Two as well, and then a light olive green in the Three, golden in the Four, and seems to settle down to a more realistic blue for the rest of the suit all the way to the King.

This is the gift of Fire, of life itself, the basic energy without which nothing could happen. The phallic stick suggests male sexuality and potency, a good card for the man in a couple trying to get pregnant. But we can go beyond that and describe it as the life force in general, that which allows us to take action or even want to take action. As the first card of the first suit of the Minor Arcana, it signifies beginnings and first impulses.

Eight leaves fall, the number of Strength. They subtly form the Hebrew letter yod ('; see also the Tower and the Aces of Cups and Swords), the first letter of the divine name (see the Wheel of Fortune and Temperance). Yod signifies pure energy. At the other end of the suit, the single stick will have multiplied into ten burdens, but here the desire to act remains pure.

· · · · · ·

DIVINATORY MEANINGS:

Energy, life, good health, forcefulness,

enthusiastic beginnings.

REVERSED:

Hesitation, setbacks, doubt. Possibly not the time to

begin something new. For a man, possible issues around

sexuality (depending on the question and other cards).

Two of Wands

ELEMENT:

fire

THEME:

choice, balance

We see an accomplished, successful man on what seems to be the wall of a castle, though his clothes give him the look of a merchant, not a nobleman. He holds a globe in his hand, as if he has conquered the world—except it's a very small world, and now he seems to look beyond it to the larger one. The choice here becomes whether to stay with what he has or to risk his security for the advantages of new experience.

He holds a stick, as if ready to set out, but the second remains bolted to the wall, symbolic of what holds him in his current life—maybe responsibility, family, prestige.

Waite describes him as having "the sadness of Alexander [the Great]," who wept because he had conquered the (known) world, and what was left? But maybe that is both too grand and a little too harsh. The way he looks out suggests he knows full well there is more to life than his own small world of success or power, but how much does he want to risk? Can he walk away from everything he's done, and maybe his responsibilities to others, to fulfill the Wands' desire for adventure? On the stone to the left we see an emblem of roses crossed by lilies, the same flowers found on the Magician's arbor. They signify the purity of his desire.

· · · · · ·

DIVINATORY MEANINGS:

Choice, especially between security and adventure. Issues of risk. Success but also feelings of being closed in.

REVERSED:

A move into new territory in a person's life. Consequences of a choice. Excitement but also nervousness.

Three of Wands

ELEMENT:
fire

THEME:
the flowering energy of the suit

People often ask about the difference between the Two and Three of Wands. Both stand on a high place looking out over water; both hold out a wand. One subtle difference—in the Two, the man holds one wand, with the other wand bolted to the wall. Here, two of the three wands stand on their own, as if something has taken root. And where the man in the Two looks out from a castle wall, this figure stands out in the open, beyond security or shelter. Look at his clothes. Do they appear wealthy or are they a patchwork? Maybe he is willing to risk everything for the sake of Wands' fiery desire for adventure and new possibility. In this way, the elemental energy "flowers" and takes hold.

He stands with his back to us, his face carefully hidden, like the child in Judgement. This suggests new and unknown worlds. Unlike the child, he stands alone, so that the card sometimes indicates taking a chance on something new without partners or support. His position—alone on a hill—implies the Hermit but maybe also the Fool.

Look carefully at the bay below him. Do you see the boats moving through the water? Their small size shows how high up he stands, how far removed he is from the actual events taking place below. Some say he's literally missed the boat—life is taking place without him due to his reluctance to get involved. But maybe they're *his* boats, a fleet under his command. You might ask yourself or the querent whether the boats are sailing out or returning.

. . . . . .

DIVINATORY MEANINGS:

Standing alone, looking out on your life. Committing
all your resources to something. Alternatively, a
reluctance to get involved, especially in relationships.

REVERSED:

An old fortunetelling tradition says "the end of adversity."
Possibly joining with others or partnership in business.

Four of Wands

ELEMENT:
fire

THEME:
structure

For many people this is one of the happiest cards in Tarot, so positive that Waite says of the reversed position, "The meaning remains unaltered." We see a group celebration, two figures in the foreground raising bouquets of flowers while others dance behind them. The four sticks strung together with flowers remind some people of a wedding canopy such as the Jewish chuppah, so the card hints at marriage, especially when it appears with such cards as the Lovers, the Two of Cups, or the Hierophant (who officiates at weddings). Others reject this because they see the two figures in front as both women, though Smith's famously androgynous style makes it hard to say, and indeed that distinction has become less and less important. Tarot card meanings do change with the times, whatever the creators' original intent.

The number 4 evokes structure, but the nature of Fire acts against containment. Add to this that Mercy, the fourth position on the Tree of Life, represents expansiveness, and we see the simplest possible structure. Notice they have left a much more solid structure, a gray walled city. This can mean something as simple as a block party or as profound as recovery from a long illness. If we place this alongside the Tower, also made of gray stone, we might notice that the people appear similar, one in red, one in blue (the primary masculine and feminine colors). Thus the card can suggest getting free of some difficult situation before it builds up to an explosion. As with Judgement, the primary figures' liberation brings joy to those around them.

· · · · · ·

DIVINATORY MEANINGS:

Celebration and joy, especially with others.
Possibly a wedding. Recovery from illness
or release from a difficult situation.

REVERSED:

Following Waite, the meaning remains unchanged.
Also prosperity, life in the country,
possibly a delayed celebration.

Five of Wands

ELEMENT:
fire

THEME:
difficulties

Fire dramatically surges with life and optimism. Thus the element goes against the number 5, which in the Rider cards show difficulties and struggle. The Fives test us and hopefully make us stronger or wiser. Nietzsche's famous line "what doesn't kill me makes me stronger" might be a credo for Fire faced with hard circumstances. The group celebration of Four gives way to conflict as five boys or young men fight with sticks.

Or do they? This is one of those cards where we need to ask ourselves or the querent, "What is going on here?" Are they fighting? If so, no one seems to be getting hurt. They may remind us of children who pretend to sword fight with sticks but just bang them together without trying to hurt anyone. The card may indicate a situation of good-natured conflict or competition, where everyone acts fairly, driven more by the excitement of the competition than a desire to destroy anyone.

Some people say they are trying to build something. If so, the anarchic Fire energy makes it difficult to coordinate their actions. The card can stand for chaotic energy in an organization.

. . . . . .

DIVINATORY MEANINGS:

Competition without rancor. Positive but chaotic
energy in need of organization or direction.
Enthusiasm without clear direction.

REVERSED:

Learning how to focus energy or direct enthusiasm in
productive ways. Sometimes a competitive situation,
such as a workplace turning nasty and people acting
unethically or doing something behind the querent's back.

Six of Wands

ELEMENT:
fire

THEME:
unequal relationship, generosity

The Five of Wands showed us enthusiastic but chaotic energy, with everything equal but nothing getting done. Here we see a leader, and the theme of unequal relationships shows that someone with positive Wands energy can attract willing followers. We see him on a horse while others walk alongside as though part of a parade, an image we also get from the decorative cloth covering the horse.

While the five walkers' Wands all appear more or less the same height, his rises above them, showing his superiority. Generosity here means taking the role of confident leader so that others can organize around him.

The Hermetic Order of the Golden Dawn gave titles to each of the Minor cards, and they called the Six of Wands "Victory." We see two laurel wreaths, one on his head, the other displayed on his Wand. But has the conquest already happened, or does his supreme confidence just take victory for granted? Waite says "the crown of hope" and "expectation crowned with its own desire." Thus the card takes on the quality of a self-fulfilling prophecy. Believe in yourself enough, assume you will get what you seek, and not only will it happen, but others will also expect you to triumph.

But we might ask how someone develops that level of self-confidence. If we try to pretend we have it, then it won't work. The cards, however, do not just show us things that would be a good idea; they show us things that are possible. And we can use the image itself—looking at it, absorbing it—to bring us confidence and leadership.

· · · · · ·

DIVINATORY MEANINGS:

Confidence, success, optimism, leadership.
The ability to attract followers. Victory in
something as a self-fulfilling prophecy.

REVERSED:

*Negativity, pessimism, self-doubt. The challenge
becomes to work with the image right-side up in order
to turn yourself around. A more positive interpretation:
going your own way without need of followers.*

Seven of Wands

ELEMENT:
fire

THEME:
action

We would expect that as the most active suit, Wands would take the theme of action almost to an extreme. And certainly he appears energetic, standing in a wide stance on top of a hill, holding his stick as if ready for combat. Because of his posture, most people assume the wands below are thrusting up at him in some kind of attack, almost as if the followers from the Six have turned against the leader they so eagerly marched alongside. But, of course, there are other interpretations, including the idea of extra resources. The face here appears more expressive than on many of the cards. But what exactly does it show? Determination? Anger? Fear? Excitement? This is one of the cards where it can really help to ask the querent to describe the picture, especially the attitude of the central figure.

Notice the mismatched shoe and boot, as if he got dressed in such a hurry he just grabbed what he could find and ran up the hill. That lack of organization suggests someone struggling just to stay on top of things, handling several crises at once. In other words, this card can seem uncomfortably close to many people's lives.

Every suit carries an advantage and a flaw. Wands possess all that energy and optimism, but Fire resists containment and thus can find it hard to make plans or choose its battles. If indeed the man here represents a fighter, he seems stuck in six battles at once, without a clear plan of how to resolve them.

. . . . . .

DIVINATORY MEANINGS:

*Dynamic energy, possibly aggressive or defensive against real
(or imagined) threats. Someone who puts energy into many
different things at once but has trouble resolving any of them.*

REVERSED:

*Disorganization, possibly feeling overwhelmed.
Alternatively, learning to choose battles or
to work on one problem at a time.*

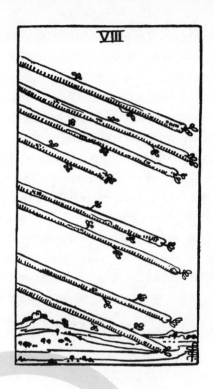

Eight of Wands

ELEMENT:

fire

THEME:

movement

Aside from the aces, where we see only hands without bodies, this card is the only one in the entire Minor Arcana without any people. In fact, if we think of the animals on the Moon and the mythological figures on the Wheel of Fortune, this becomes the only card in the whole deck without any creatures (there are at least hands on the aces), other than the scattered trees in the landscape. What do we make of this lack of people? We might consider it events that happen of their own accord, without the need of any deliberate action by the querent or anyone else. This might seem comforting or disturbing, depending on which way those events turn out.

The theme of movement goes well with fiery Wands. Maybe we don't see any people because Fire energy just takes over. There is no chaos here; the wands move together all in the same direction, the same angle. The placement of the leaves shows that they travel from left to right and toward the earth. The left side traditionally represents potential, and the right, actualization. Similarly, movement toward the ground suggests that events will come to some fruition. Possibilities are moving toward reality. The peaceful landscape suggests a positive result.

One nice tradition about this card calls it "the arrows of love." Does the querent send or receive them? Either way, the positive energy of the card suggests the arrows will reach a welcome heart.

· · · · · ·

DIVINATORY MEANINGS:

Positive movement, organization, swift action with good results. Expression of love, either as messages or simply desire.

REVERSED:

Delays, lack of focus. Plans might need more conscious guidance to bring results. Possibly arrows of jealousy that, with other problem cards, could endanger a relationship.

Nine of Wands

ELEMENT:

fire

THEME:

intensity, high degree

This card resembles the Seven in a number of ways. He stands courageously, battered but ready to defend whatever matters most to him. At the same time, like the Seven, we don't get much sense of solutions, only the strength to continue his battles. As Fire reaches the higher numbers, the weaknesses of the suit become more prominent—lack of organization, lack of alternative ways to solve problems, too much reliance on courage and strength, and a willingness to take on problems.

When this card comes up, we might ask the querent—or ourselves, even if we have a usual interpretation—to consider the sticks behind him. The way he seems to glance over his shoulder at them suggests they might be problems, or even enemies, against which he stands ready once more to defend himself. But notice the gap right behind him, as if the stick he holds was part of the line-up just a moment ago. We might see the wands as, in fact, all belonging to him: his arsenal of resources or reserves of energy.

The picture is a model of tension. The way he grips the stick not only hunches up his right shoulder, it also covers his heart and lungs, making it hard to feel or breathe easily. The bandage around his head indicates a psychic wound, the price he's paid for his heroic stance against life's problems.

· · · · · ·

DIVINATORY MEANINGS:

Power, courage, the ability to defend yourself against attack or just a series of crises. Defensiveness, tension.

REVERSED:

Weakness but also giving up a defensive attitude. Can indicate a willingness to find alternative solutions rather than constantly battle. Openness to other people's perspectives or needs. (If you choose not to work with reversed meanings, consider these meanings as inherent in the card, along with the right–side up ones.)

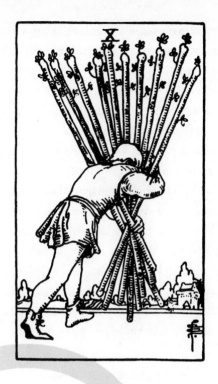

Ten of Wands

ELEMENT:
fire

THEME:
excess

For Wands, an excess of Fire can result in an excess of bur-dens. All that enthusiasm from the Ace here spreads into ten sticks that the figure—whose face is hidden by his bowed head—now must carry to his destination. It's as if his fiery confidence led him to accept more and more responsibility. He may be a person who simply cannot resist an opportunity or a challenge or has a belief that everything depends on him, and somehow he cannot ask anyone else to take any responsibility.

Nor does he stop to work out the best way to resolve his issues or find solutions. In a class once, I joked that this picture shows that Pamela Smith never had to carry ten sticks anywhere, since his task would become easier if he would bundle them together on his shoulder. But someone pointed out that that would crush all the buds, and he's willing to make his work harder so that all the possibilities have a chance to bloom; thus he becomes the image of dedication to others' needs.

In a relationship reading, the Ten of Wands indicates someone who attempts to keep the relationship going all by her- or himself, asking nothing of the partner. Usually this hints at a fear of rejection. "If I ask him to change his habits or communicate more, he'll just leave."

• • • • • •

DIVINATORY MEANINGS:

Burdens, too much responsibility. Enthusiasm that's led to someone taking on too many projects. In relationship readings, someone who attempts to keep the relationship going all alone.

REVERSED:

Can mean failure of projects but more often means a release of responsibilities. Simplifying your life, either because projects end or because you share the burdens. In relationships, greater communication and sharing of problems.

A READING FOR
The Suit of Wands

1

2   3

4

1. What is the fire in my life?

2. How am I passionate?

3. How do I burn myself out?

4. How can I direct my fire?

Cups

ACE of CUPS.

ELEMENT:
water

THEME:
pure energy of suit, gift

A white hand emerges from a cloud, gracefully holding
out an elaborate Cup, as if presenting it to us. More
elegant than all but that held by the queen, it represents the
Holy Grail, the cup supposedly used by Christ at the Last Sup-
per, and thus given magical healing power. The Grail stories
emerged in the Middle Ages, entwined with King Arthur and

135

chivalry, but they had a strong revival around the time the Rider deck was created, with some people claiming that the four Tarot suit emblems were derived from the Grail's "hallows," sacred objects described in the mystical stories. If we had any doubts that this Ace shows us the Grail, the dove—an image of the Holy Spirit—bearing a communion wafer would make it clear. And yet, many people believe that the hallows themselves come from objects sacred to pre-Christian gods and goddesses, with the Grail originally a cauldron of rebirth.

Each ace comes to us as a gift, something not earned but just there. The Ace of Cups is the purest gift, for it is the gift of love. As well as romantic and emotional love, it also symbolizes spiritual love, even divine grace, but also healing. The water overflows the cup in five streams, the Major Arcana plus the four suits. The drops of water form the Hebrew letter yod, the beginning of the all-powerful name of God and itself a symbol of grace. Notice there is very little land in the picture, mostly water, pure feeling.

· · · · · ·

DIVINATORY MEANINGS:

Love (on many levels). Grace, healing, spiritual
awareness. Emotional and spiritual nourishment.
All these things come as a gift—simply there, without
our having to struggle or fight for them.

REVERSED:

Happiness may be blocked or we might not recognize love when someone offers it to us. A need to nourish yourself physically, emotionally, and spiritually.

Two of Cups

ELEMENT:

water

THEME:

choice, balance

I n Cups, the suit of feeling and relationship, the theme of balance comes through a union of equals. Though the man reaches out to the woman, they both wear wreaths and stand with formal solemnity. In fact, they appear so serious that some people do not see them as a romantic couple at all, but rather as magicians performing a ritual. This idea becomes reinforced by the caduceus that rises between their cups. The ancient image of two snakes wound around a staff can represent male and female energies entwined, but also the energy called kundalini, pictured as two snakes coiled at the base of the spine. When the kundalini awakens, it rises, entwined, along the spine—solar and lunar energy mixed together. The esoteric view of this card gets a boost from the alchemical image of the winged lion head that tops the caduceus. (The use of the caduceus as the medical symbol probably derives from confusion with the healing rod of Asclepius the physician-god, a stick with one snake wound around it.)

Despite the clear magical imagery, the Two of Cups most often signifies a relationship, often a new one but serious. It can mean a commitment in a relationship and sometimes a renewal of an old one.

· · · · · · ·

DIVINATORY MEANINGS:

A relationship, possibly a new one but meaningful.
Renewal of love; commitment. Any flow of energy between
two people, mental or magical as well as emotional.
Possibly yoga or spiritual practices that raise kundalini.

REVERSED:

A relationship becomes less significant than originally
expected. Friends rather than lovers. Old issues may
block new love. With the Hermit, High Priestess, or
other reversed love cards, a need to be on your own.

Three of Cups

ELEMENT:

water

THEME:

the flowering energy of the suit

One of the happiest cards in the deck, the Three of Cups
shows celebration, joy, and the sharing of good times
with friends or family. Those hoping for signs of romance may
be disappointed, since the card indicates a more communal
love, but the image is, above all, joyous. The scene appears to

be harvest time, with pumpkins on the ground, and thus is a scene of abundance. Harvests do not just happen, they come after a spring and summer of hard work, so this card can symbolize a great effort rewarded, yet the emphasis remains on the celebration. It can mean something as simple as a great party or an evening with close friends.

Because it shows three women, it embodies Water's feminine, flowing energy. It also suggests the many images of three goddesses, such as the three Graces, the three Fates, and the Maiden-Mother-Crone of ancient (and modern) worship. Thus the card gives us feminine qualities of deep emotional bonds and intense sharing.

And there's something more: look at the positions of the three cups, and then look at the Tree of Life (seen on the Ten of Pentacles). The cups subtly form the top triangle of the Tree, while the women themselves, seemingly dancing freely, actually form the Tree itself, with its three vertical columns. In the Minor Arcana, the spiritual underlies daily life.

• • • • • • •

DIVINATORY MEANINGS:

Joy, celebration, family, friendship. Deep bonds, especially (but not only) between women. Good times, especially after hard work brings a good "harvest."

REVERSED:

Possible strains between friends. Alternatively, a friendship may turn into a romance. A need to take action on your own or delay celebration until something important is finished.

Four of Cups

ELEMENT:
water

THEME:
structure

How do we structure emotions? One answer this card might give us is to hold them within and not respond to new possibilities. The "hero" of this picture sits with his arms crossed steadfastly against his chest, seemingly staring at three cups lined up in front of him while a mysterious hand emerges from a cloud to offer something new. This is the only card out-side the aces where we see such an image, and so it suggests that what he ignores is love or feeling or possibly an exciting new opportunity.

Many people attach a sort of moral lesson to this card. "You're ignoring something important," they might say, or "You have to uncross your arms and reach out for that cup of love." Well, maybe—but if that was the lesson, wouldn't the card show him doing that? Sometimes, in fact, we might need to learn *not* to take every new opportunity, whether emotional or a new project. If someone says "How are you?" do you usu-ally answer "Oh, crazy busy"? This card can remind us to pro-tect ourselves from grabbing at every new thing, but that, too, is just one way to look at it.

There is a curious connection between the Three, Four, and Five of Cups, a progression of loss. The Three shows rejoic-ing, the cups held high. Here, three cups stand in a group as he stares at them, alone. In the Five, something has knocked them over.

· · · · · ·

DIVINATORY MEANINGS:

Detachment; an opportunity either not seen or ignored.
Someone may be in love with the querent, and the querent
does not realize it. Hesitation about trying something new.

REVERSED:

Here we do emphasize taking the cup. It may
involve a risk or seeing an offer—love or
opportunity—that was previously ignored.

Five of Cups

ELEMENT:

water

THEME:

difficulties

Cups are probably the happiest suit, with images of love, family joy, and celebration. When we come to the difficult Five, however, we see what most people consider an image of sorrow and loss. The three cups that we saw raised high in the Three of Cups, then simply stared at in the Four, now have fallen over. Perhaps by ignoring love we risk its ultimate loss. The curious red and green liquids that have poured out might suggest a failed alchemical process, but in most situations they symbolize sorrow—about what, we cannot really say.

Do you see this person as a man or a woman? Does it matter? He (or she) stands tightly wrapped in a black cloak, as if she (or he) wants no other feelings to penetrate grief. Some see this as a card of mourning, and if it appears with such cards as Death or the Nine of Swords, we need to acknowledge the possibility of some great loss. As always, however, we should hesitate greatly before predicting physical death. There are many other losses a person might face.

Notice the two cups standing behind the figure. They may signify what hasn't been lost or spilled. Readers sometimes tell the querent to turn around, see what good things remain, pick them up, and cross over the bridge to continue life. But, as with the Four, if that was the idea, the picture would show it. Sometimes we need to experience the full force of our grief.

· · · · · · ·

DIVINATORY MEANINGS:

Loss, sadness, regret. Recognition of something not appreciated until it has ended. Someone wrapped in grief, not seeing what remains.

REVERSED:

Here it does become valuable to consider the two cups left standing. Recognition of something valuable. Going on with life after a loss.

Six of Cups

ELEMENT:
water

THEME:
unequal relationship, generosity

On the surface this seems like a happy and simple card, the very image of the Six's theme of generosity, as what appears to be an older child gives a flower to a young girl. Other than the Ace, with its overflowing water, and the Page of Cups, with his fish (and the fantasy images of the Seven), this is the only card where the cups actually contain something. The flowers and the houses suggest grounding Cups' emotion in reality.

Yet many people have found something strange, even sinister, in this card. It embodies that other idea of Six, unequal relationship, for the figure on the left looms over the girl (compare the equal figures in the Two of Cups). And notice how overdressed she appears, her hand encased in a large mitten despite the seemingly warm day. Some see the card as showing someone as powerless as the tied-up woman in the Eight of Swords, just not as obvious.

Most interpretations see this card as nostalgia, a look back at a happy childhood or just happiness from some earlier point, such as the beginning of a relationship. Nostalgia can be deceptive—a fantasy that sometimes can cover up an unpleasant history. Some see the card as denial. The clothes the figures wear, especially the one on the left, look like a fairy tale. We may think of fairy tales as sweet stories, but they often take us to dark, fearful places before they get to happily ever after.

· · · · · ·

DIVINATORY MEANINGS:

More mixed than other cards, depending on whether
we see the card as simple happiness or having dark
undercurrents. Most common meaning is nostalgia
for an earlier time, especially childhood. Passivity.
Allowing others to be in charge or take care of you.

REVERSED:

Focus on present situations, rejecting nostalgia and passivity.
An honest look at childhood, perhaps healing childhood pain.

Seven of Cups

ELEMENT:

water

THEME:

action

Afigure with his back to us, in silhouette but seemingly awestruck, stares at seven cups that appear in the clouds. Unlike the Ace or, for that matter, the Four, no hand emerges to offer him anything; the cups just rise in the air before him. Wonders fill them—treasures, a castle, a snake *and* a dragon, a wreath of honor, and a mysterious veiled figure as well as a beautiful head unattached to a body. What does it all mean? Why does a skull appear on the cup with the laurel wreath?

Water's qualities of flowing emotion do not really go well with the Seven's theme of action. The action here takes place entirely in the imagination, unconnected to any ground of reality. The images may link to actual situations, or maybe ideas—a Tarotist named Carolyn Guss sees the seven figures as emblematic of the seven planetary spheres (Sun, Moon, Mercury, Venus, Mars, Jupiter, Saturn)—but what does he do to bring them to reality? (Another theory sees them as the seven vices.)

All this makes the Seven yet another Cups card people want to fix. They may say, "You have to make a choice and take action." (The passive and emotional Cups cards tend to bring out such reactions.) But maybe fantasies are exactly what a person needs. We can't change our lives unless we first allow ourselves to imagine other possibilities.

· · · · · · ·

DIVINATORY MEANINGS:

Imagination, fantasies, wonder. Passivity; no action to make the fantasies real. If action cards follow, the fantasies may lead to some big change. Possibly hallucinations.

REVERSED:

Taking action on fantasies. Making a choice out of many possibilities. Telling people your desires or dreams.

Eight of Cups

ELEMENT:
water

THEME:
movement

A cloaked figure walks up a hill under a full moon. He may remind us of the Hermit, who is aligned with the Moon (the Moon's number, 18, reduces, 1+8, to 9) and who stands on a hill holding a similar staff. Like the Hermit, he can be leaving the world of ordinary activities to seek some higher truth.

Unlike in the Five of Cups, nothing here has been knocked over, nothing spilled. He simply knows that the time has come to let go of something, to move on. This card can show you the moment when you know you need to end a relationship, quit a job, move house, or make some other change in your life. Notice the gap in the top row of cups. Maybe he's gone to find something that was missing from his life.

On a less dramatic level, it can mean a time to move away from outer activities toward solitude or inner reflection. This does not have to be a long-term change. Tarot readings show us the way things are right now, and things can change quickly. Look again at the way the Moon is shown. Rather than a scene at night, the card may show us a solar eclipse. Symbolically this means lunar qualities taking over from solar, at least for a time. Look in at yourself rather than out at the world. Let your intuition guide you rather than try to solve problems.

· · · · · · ·

DIVINATORY MEANINGS:

Recognition that it's time to leave something, to move on. There is no disaster, only an inner awareness of change. Less dramatically, it can indicate a time to be quiet, to look inward; possibly to consider a higher purpose beyond your ordinary activities.

REVERSED:

This is not the time to leave something. Instead, recognize the value of a situation and see how you can improve it. More simply, it may be a time to return from solitude to a greater involvement with other people and the world around you.

Nine of Cups
ELEMENT:
water

THEME:
intensity, high degree

A richly dressed, portly man sits on a bench before a table with nine cups lined up. Are they trophies of his success? Maybe we can imagine him as the journeyer from the Eight who went off to find the missing cup from that top row and now has returned with the sense that life is complete. Or is it?

Does he seem shallow in his satisfaction, or even defensive? The way he crosses his arms, with the hands on the forearms, is not a relaxed posture; try it.

A fortunetelling tradition revived by modern Tarotists calls the Nine of Cups the "Wish Card." If it appears anywhere in the reading, the querent gets whatever he or she desires. Clearly, this makes it a card most people want to see.

Waite's primary meanings for this card *reversed* may give us a clue to our general understanding. "Truth, loyalty, liberty," he says, though he also adds "mistakes, imperfections." It's as if the figure gives up his line of successes, his trophies and comfortable life, and seeks something deeper. When we let go of comfort and search for meaning or strong experience, we often do make mistakes, maybe even make fools (or Fools) of ourselves.

Some people have focused on the curtain. Does it hide secrets? Challenges? New opportunities or temptations? And what mistakes might he make if he takes a chance on a new life?

• • • • • •

DIVINATORY MEANINGS:

Wishes granted. Success and satisfaction, though perhaps on an outer level. Shallowness, smugness. Pleasure. Possibly finding something that was missing from life.

REVERSED:

Following Waite, the virtues of truth and loyalty over personal satisfaction. Liberty from material possessions. Possible mistakes. Hidden things revealed.

Ten of Cups

ELEMENT:
water

THEME:
excess

Cups, in many ways, is the happiest of the four suits, and an excess of Water gives us this joyous image, as if the divine grace of the Ace has fulfilled its promise with this happy family. The man and woman stand entwined, their arms raised as if they form one person (notice that, as in Judgement, the man stands on the left, the woman on the right). They look up at the rainbow that holds the cups of their spiritual happiness, conscious of their blessings, while alongside them the children dance joyously, without cares or worries.

This is the happiest of the tens, certainly compared to Wands or Swords but probably to Pentacles as well—the people there seem far more prosperous. Compared to their manorlike home with its several buildings, this card shows only a modest little house, the roof painted red for passion. But if you look at the people in both cards, who would you rather be?

We could also compare this card to the Nine, where the cups stand like trophies of success compared to the Ten's vision in the sky. The merchant there appears richer than this family, but he's alone. The Seven fantasized about a different life. The Eight went seeking what was missing. The Nine and Ten show two paths of what we might find and create for ourselves.

. . . . . .

DIVINATORY MEANINGS:

Happiness and fulfillment, especially with family or relationships. Spiritual values over material values. A good omen for marriage or couples hoping to have children.

REVERSED:

Difficulty appreciating what we have. Dissatisfaction. Something may threaten or call into question someone's happiness. Possible money problems.

A READING FOR
The Suit of Cups

1

2   3

4   5

6

1. How am I emotional?

2. How do I express my feelings to others?

3. How do I hide my feelings?

4. What is my emotional history?

5. How does my emotional history
   affect my life now?

6. How can I find and develop love?

Swords

ACE of SWORDS.

ELEMENT:
air

THEME:
the pure energy of the suit, a gift

A white hand emerges from a cloud to tightly grip a double-edged sword, as if this particular symbol is hard to keep steady. The element for Swords, Air, refers to the mind and clear thought that can cut through confusion. The very object, however, is a weapon that can bring great sorrow, and this double edge cuts through the entire suit. The familiar yods here take the form of drops of golden light. We see only six, three on each side, as if to balance the two "gifts," rather than the outpouring on the Aces of Wands and Cups. Similarly, we find a remote, even bleak, mountain landscape below the sword, symbolic of the great heights the mind can reach but also the remoteness from ordinary life.

Only three swords in the Rider deck point straight up: the Ace, the Queen, and Justice. They signify commitment to truth, rather than what we might want or believe. The connection to Justice can imply a need to use this gift justly, though it seems removed from ordinary things. The crown, with its leaves of honor, may signify the success and respect most of us see as the goals of life. The sword penetrates to a higher level, as if the pure mind reaches beyond ordinary goals.

. . . . . .

DIVINATORY MEANINGS:

The gift of clear thought, spiritual truth, and higher values, even if these can bring sorrow. Singleness of mind and purpose. Possibly a challenge to act justly.

REVERSED:

Confusion, difficulty thinking clearly. Possibly a strong mind that can be manipulative.

Two of Swords

ELEMENT:

air

THEME:

choice, balance

With swords held at her shoulders, a blindfolded woman in a dress as gray as her surroundings sits on a stone bench in front of a pool of water. The theme of balance seems tentative here, as if the mind can only stay at peace by closing off options and especially communication. The Swords suit contains two blindfolded women, who may seem similar but have a great difference. The tied-up woman of the Eight cannot remove the covering from her eyes, but this woman seems to have blindfolded herself deliberately; if she wanted, she could just put down the swords and take it off.

One way to look at her is as someone closed off from other people. Who would dare approach her, with those blades ready to strike blindly at anyone who comes close? Her posture covers—closes off—the vulnerable heart and lungs. And yet, this is not something easily maintained, for the swords are heavy, and they raise her center of gravity so that if something did come close, it could knock her backwards into the choppy waters of emotion.

But consider it in a different way: swords can signify purity of thought. We might see this card as a commitment to meditation or some other spiritual pursuit. The blindfold shuts out distractions, while the crossed arms and swords help focus her attention. Her number, 2, links her to the High Priestess.

· · · · · ·

DIVINATORY MEANINGS:

Someone who doesn't want to see something or who closes off
emotions. Isolation from people in your life. Alternatively
(especially with the High Priestess or Hermit), turning
toward a spiritual path or putting all your energy into a task.

REVERSED:

Becoming involved with others. Dropping defenses.
Possibly lack of focus in spiritual or practical goals.

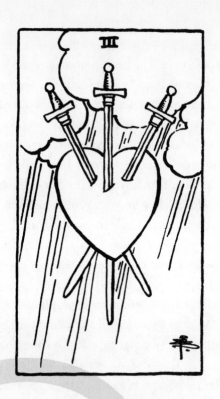

Three of Swords

ELEMENT:

air

THEME:

the flowering energy of the suit

One of the Minor Arcana's simplest, most direct pictures, it shows no land, no people, only a heart (or, really, the abstract symbol of a heart—an actual heart looks nothing like this) pierced by three swords while rain slants down. If we take the sorrowful energy of Swords and let it "flower," this is what comes to us. Despite the lack of figures, most people who look at this card get the message: heartbreak, sorrow, grief.

And yet there is something more here, as it seems with so many of the Swords cards. The picture carries a certain balance, a calm acceptance. The hilts of the swords form the top triangle of the Tree of Life, while the points suggest places seven, eight, and nine. Four and five form the peaks of the heart, with six the place where the swords meet as they pierce the center. What's missing is the tenth position—thus ten, the place of the physical world, of events, lies *below* the picture, as if the sorrow has become detached from what caused it and exists in a pure state. The third place on the Tree of Life bears the title Understanding, and this picture can hint at just that— understanding our suffering, not just of any particular event, but maybe of life itself.

All this can seem little comfort to a grim picture, but sometimes if we allow ourselves to take our pain into our hearts, we can raise it up and find healing.

· · · · · ·

DIVINATORY MEANINGS:

Sorrow, heartbreak, a deep sadness. Calm acceptance
that allows us to go beyond grief and find healing.

REVERSED:

Recovery from sorrow, release of pain. Alternatively, trying
to avoid suffering. Denial or closing off emotions. Which
way it goes depends on the reading and the cards around it.

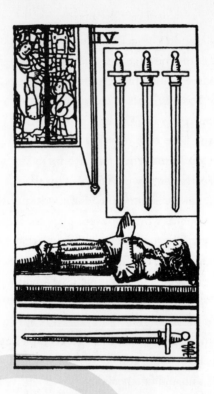

Four of Swords

ELEMENT:

air

THEME:

structure

Waite and Gray both see this as an effigy. Most modern readers view him as a knight asleep in a church with a stained glass window showing a worshipper kneeling before Christ. In the window, the word *Pax*, Latin for "peace," appears in a halo above Christ's head. Three swords are mounted to the wall, pointing at the knight's head (third eye, actually, seat of psychic opening), throat (communication), and solar plexus (deep knowledge). They are not threatening so much as activating these powerful centers. A fourth sword lies beneath him.

Air finds structure even more difficult than Fire or Water. How can we contain the air? How can we give a fixed shape to our thoughts? The knight may be not so much asleep as lying in deep meditation, for no one's hands would stay that way once he falls asleep. Thus the card can indicate a withdrawal from struggle to find quiet, inner peace, and possibly healing; on a simpler level, perhaps it indicates a break from a period of tension.

Sometimes if we withdraw too much from engagement with other people and the world, we can become isolated and in need of someone to reach out to us and bring us back. The mysterious knight may remind us of such figures as Sleeping Beauty, who could not awake by herself, or the Fisher King of the Grail stories, who lay in a coma until a pure knight came to heal him.

· · · · · ·

DIVINATORY MEANINGS:

Rest, withdrawal from struggle, inner peace. Meditation or some other spiritual practice that involves turning attention inward to awaken our deeper senses. Possibly isolation or closing down emotionally to avoid pain.

REVERSED:

A return to activity. Renewed energy. Could be a healing, physically or emotionally.

Five of Swords

ELEMENT:
air

THEME:
difficulties

The theme of difficulties fits Swords perfectly. Here we see a rough scene with sharp-edged clouds and choppy water. A red-haired man, dressed largely in red—the color of the planet Mars, named for the god of war—dominates two others, smirking in triumph as he holds three of the swords. We might assume that the two swords on the ground belonged to the two figures who walk away defeated. One of the two, the farthest away, seems to weep, but the other appears calmer, as if he had decided the fight wasn't worth it against someone so powerful and has dropped his sword, withdrawing.

The way we interpret this card may depend on who we see as the main figure, the "hero" of the scene. Smith probably meant her picture to illustrate Waite's meanings of "degradation, destruction," and other harsh things. This assumes that we see ourselves in the figures who leave the scene. The red-haired man looms so large because of our sense of helplessness or shame. But what if we see ourselves as that largest figure? Does the card turn around and become a message, or even a prediction, of triumph? Maybe. But then we could ask what kind of person is this, and do we really want to become him?

In readings regarding conflicts, especially lawsuits, be on your guard if this card comes up with Justice reversed.

· · · · · ·

DIVINATORY MEANINGS:

Defeat or possibly an unprincipled victory. Alternatively,
choosing to walk away from a fight you cannot win.
Stormy situations, possibly family quarrels.

REVERSED:

Moving beyond some disturbing loss or defeat. A new
beginning. Communication may replace hostility.

Six of Swords

ELEMENT:

air

THEME:

unequal relationship, generosity

Whenever I think of the way Pamela Colman Smith's drawings reach beyond their "official" meanings, this card comes to mind. Waite says "journey by water," and clearly we see a voyage in a boat. But the picture evokes mystery and depth. Who are these people: a ferryman and his passengers? A family? If we take the wrapped figure as a woman, why does she sit so hunched over, with her child pressed close against her?

This type of boat, called a punt, was used by ferrymen to carry passengers across a river. The most famous example, often shown holding a black pole to push his boat across the River Styx, was Charon, the Greek ferryman who carried souls from the world of the living to the land of the dead. Should we see this card, with its shrouded woman, as a fearful omen of death?

Nothing in the card's traditional meanings suggests this. Instead, we might see her as damped down—if not dead emotionally, then unwilling to raise her head or cast off her cloak. There is an air of silence about this card, as though none of the figures are willing to talk and instead continue on their journey.

And the swords—do they symbolize the pain the people carry with them? Sad memories? Waite notes that they don't seem to weigh much. But they ride in front, more prominent than the people themselves.

• • • • • •

DIVINATORY MEANINGS:

Waite's "journey by water" remains a simple
fortunetelling possibility. More subtly, people (especially
families) who carry pain or secrets in their lives
and do not share them. Silence; things hidden.

REVERSED:

Speaking up, revealing family secrets. Disrupting some
long-standing situation. This can produce conflict or anxiety
but ultimately lead to freedom, especially from the past.

Seven of Swords

ELEMENT:

air

THEME:

action

In recent years this card has taken on a very specific meaning: an illicit sexual affair. We get this from the way he tiptoes from the tent, but also just the way he seems so pleased with himself, and just perhaps the way he makes off with the phallic swords, as if secretly taking the power from his lover's husband. No card automatically means one thing, especially something so definite. Still, if this Seven comes up, you might keep this particular "action" in the back of your mind in case other cards or the situation support it.

More generally we get the sense of someone who acts alone, very pleased with himself. The card conveys trickiness, cleverness—an action of the mind, but not especially great success, for it seems to lack planning. He makes off with five of the swords but leaves two behind. Nor has he caused any actual harm to anyone. The small silhouetted group on the lower left take no notice of him. We can imagine them returning to their tents and scratching their heads as they wonder what happened to their swords.

This card appears as the most active of the Swords cards, and it's also the most mental, for in occult tradition yellow indicates activity of the mind. The red boots and hat, on the other hand, suggest excitement or passion.

· · · · · ·

DIVINATORY MEANINGS:

Trickiness, cleverness, a plan that seems exciting but may not lead to long-term solutions. Impulsive action, especially done on your own. Possibly an affair.

REVERSED:

Willingness to consult with others before taking action. Getting advice. Caution; thinking twice before doing something. Resisting temptation. Possibly the end of an affair.

Eight of Swords

ELEMENT:

air

THEME:

movement

H ere we see the "other" blindfolded woman. Where the
Two of Swords figure seems to have chosen to close
herself off, this woman could not have tied herself up that
way, and so she seems more of a victim. We might recall that,

in contrast to courthouse statues, the image of Justice in the Tarot wears no blindfold, so that the character in the Eight of Swords seems to suffer some injustice. In fact, she seems the very image of female oppression, bound and helpless. A stone castle, symbol of authority, rises behind her. The phallic swords seem to surround her as she stands in mud, an image of shame. The theme of movement turns upside down to become helplessness.

But notice—no one from the castle stands guard over her. The swords do not actually block her way, nor would the pools of water really stop her. Most important, the rope does not go around her legs. What really stops her is the blindfold: mental confusion, especially that imposed by someone else. Accepting the idea of your own helplessness.

And we can see this another way. We've observed how several of the double-edged Swords cards hint at a deeper, more esoteric meaning. According to Wald and Ruth Ann Amberstone, the number of coils of rope around her match the directions for a Masonic ritual of initiation. Her helplessness might be voluntary as she seeks to go inward, away from outer consciousness to an inner revelation.

· · · · · · ·

DIVINATORY MEANINGS:

Helplessness, confusion. Feeling blocked, oppressed.
Manipulation that convinces someone she or
he has no options. Alternatively, some intense
spiritual practice to move attention inward.

REVERSED:

Discovering you have more possibilities than you thought. Clarity; seeing things in perspective. First steps to free yourself from a hard situation.

Nine of Swords

ELEMENT:
air

THEME:
intensity, high degree

One of the Rider deck's challenging images, this card shows us someone (most see her as a woman) sitting up in bed, with her hands over her face, as if weeping. Alternatively, it can mean worry, anxiety, even insomnia—whatever wakes you up in the middle of the night. Only two cards in the deck, this and the Devil, show us a completely black back-ground, and this one appears so much more *real* than the Devil, with his smiling demon lovers. Some see it as the "dark night of the soul," and this image fits the nine's theme of intensity. Notice the odd carving on the bed. It seems to show one man attacking or even killing another.

Is the emphasis all negative? Notice the bright quilt, the most colorful part of the picture. Roses for passion alternate with the signs of the zodiac, as if the cosmos itself seeks to comfort her. And maybe she *needs* to wake up and face some-thing difficult (even if she still has not taken her hands away to really see it).

The swords line up in perfect regularity, something we haven't seen since the Four. They resemble a ladder, so per-haps she can climb out of her despair by facing the truth, even though it may cut on the way.

* * * * * *

DIVINATORY MEANINGS:

Sorrow, anxiety, depression. What wakes us up in the middle of the night, including dreams or bad news. On a lighter note, insomnia.

REVERSED:

Beginnings of a recovery. Climbing out of a low point, especially facing a difficult truth.

Ten of Swords

ELEMENT:

air

THEME:

excess

Where the Nine showed us the intensity of anguish, the Ten becomes downright lurid, the very image of the theme of excess. After all, it takes only one sword to kill someone. So does this card indicate violence or even murder? To me, it suggests exaggerated mental states such as self-pity or hysteria. The focus of the Ace, with its penetration to spiritual truth, has become scattered.

We might compare the Ten to the Nine. There, the swords lined up uniformly; here, they appear at different lengths, some even crudely formed, with the hilts, or handles, at odd angles. More significantly, the complete darkness of the Nine has partly lifted to show golden light, as well as a calm lake (compare the choppy waters of the Two and Five). Tarot teacher Ellen Goldberg describes the card as a literal "golden dawn."

We've seen how some of the Swords cards (the Two, for example) lend themselves to esoteric or spiritual interpretations. Notice the hand. The fingers form the gesture of blessing that we saw in the Hierophant. We might see this as an overthrow of religious authority or orthodoxy so that people can find their own way. An alternative view is that it represents a meditation practice known as "killing the ego."

If the reading asks about medical issues, this card may indicate back problems but also the possibility of relief through acupuncture. Finally, with the Devil, it might suggest drug addiction.

▪ ▪ ▪ ▪ ▪ ▪

DIVINATORY MEANINGS:

Extreme mental states, but also the possibility that someone's fears or worries are exaggerated. Intense meditation to overcome ego. Possibly a rejection of religious authority. Medically, back problems, maybe acupuncture. With supporting cards, addiction.

REVERSED:

*Relief from suffering, as if the swords literally fall away.
Waite describes any "advantage" as "not permanent," so the
person needs to make real changes. Relief from physical pain.*

A READING FOR
The Suit of Swords

5

4

2   3

1

(In the shape of a sword pointing up, like the ace.)

1. How does my mind work?

2. How do I communicate my ideas?

3. How am I able to hear the ideas of others?

4. What do I need to learn?

5. How will I learn it?

Pentacles

ELEMENT:

earth

THEME:

the pure energy of the suit

Once again a hand emerges from a cloud, the offered pentacle held gracefully in the curve of the palm. This time no yods fall around it (see the other aces), though the hand gleams with light. With Pentacles we enter the material world, the element of Earth, and so no symbols of divine grace and mystery come to us. Here the gift becomes very real—a garden, flowers, nature civilized and gentle. Many of the cards in the suit show issues of work or money—after all, the original emblem was coins—but here we find a safe haven. We might remember that the word *paradise* derives from the Persian *paradeiza*, a walled garden, a place of beauty and sanctuary. And that a pentacle symbolizes the magic union of the heavens, the plants, and the human body.

We see an opening in the green fence toward the back of the picture, and in the distance are mountains, symbols of higher truth, the home of the Hermit. The opening, which may remind us of the wreath around the World dancer, has no gate to keep us inside or close us off from seeking something beyond the joys of the pentacle's gift. And unlike the Garden of Eden, where a flaming sword bars the way back, this sanctuary remains always open.

· · · · · ·

DIVINATORY MEANINGS:

The gift of nature, sanctuary, someplace
peaceful. Abundance, possibly money or
work, especially when truly needed.

REVERSED:

Can represent problems around money or security,
especially conflicts with others around these issues.
Leaving a safe or comfortable situation to try
something new. Starting on a spiritual path.

Two of Pentacles
ELEMENT:
earth

THEME:
choice, balance

At first glance, this appears to be one of the lighter cards in the deck. A young man wearing an odd conical hat, almost like a clown, dances a kind of jig step as he juggles, or balances, the two pentacles in a ribbon looped like an infinity sign. Behind him, ships roll up and down on cartoonlike waves. His dancing posture suggests the Fool, while the lemniscate ribbon evokes the Magician. We will see other hints of magic or mystery in daily life, especially in the arrangement of pentacles in the Five and Ten.

The question is, is he actually enjoying himself? When this card comes up, we might ask the querent to describe him and especially to look at his face. Smith's drawings are famously ambiguous, so we might view him as being focused on his juggling or maybe anxious about whether he will drop anything. And another question: does he do this just for himself or for an audience?

Since Pentacles involve work and money, and the number two the themes of choice and balance, we might remember that so many of us constantly balance—juggle—our commitments to our jobs and careers with other parts of our lives. We do this in part because of limited money but also because we don't want to have to choose one thing over another. The question then becomes how much we do it for ourselves or for others, whether we do it with grace or anxiety, and maybe whether or not we feel free to stop.

· · · · · ·

DIVINATORY MEANINGS:

Juggling aspects of work, life, or a tight budget. Maybe trying to balance practical responsibilities with relationships or entertainment. Hints of magic in daily life. The interpretation depends on whether we see him as carefree or anxious.

REVERSED:

The juggling act may end, either deliberately or because he drops something. Possibly making mistakes or finding it hard to balance career and personal life.

Three of Pentacles

earth

THEME:
the flowering energy of the suit

A sculptor works in a dim church while a monk and a master architect with the church plans seem to discuss the work. Significantly, we do not see the actual project, for the only color comes from the people; the work itself matters, not the final product. When we take the three's theme of flowering energy and apply it to Pentacles, we get the idea of mastery and creativity but also cooperation. The practical (architect) and the spiritual (monk) serve the creative, and all operate at their highest level.

The pentacles here appear as the arch of the church wall. They serve a practical purpose and at the same time form that image of the top three places on the Tree of Life, the triangle that reaches upward toward the highest truths. The architecture further calls for the triangle below to balance the upper, with a rose carved into the structure. As above, so below, with desire as the connector.

The image of three people in a church may remind us of the Hierophant with his two disciples and all those cards with one figure over two others. Here the sculptor only subtly stands higher, and only to do his work, indicating cooperation rather than hierarchy and obedience. In career readings, this card urges you to seek work at your best level but possibly also to join a partnership or group practice of some kind.

· · · · · · ·

DIVINATORY MEANINGS:

*Mastery in work. Artistry, cooperation. Working or
acting at your highest level. Satisfaction in what you
do; finding spiritual meaning in work or daily life.*

REVERSED:

*Mediocrity in work or elsewhere in daily life. Lack of
cooperation. Possibly a need to leave a job or some
other situation that doesn't allow you to do your best.*

Four of Pentacles

ELEMENT:
earth

THEME:
structure

A crowned figure sits on a simple stone bench with a city arrayed behind him. Pentacles surround him—one under each foot, one atop his head, and one cradled firmly in his arms, before his chest.

Pentacles represent the solidness of Earth, the practicality of money—issues that go well with structure, though they may act against the theme of mercy. Many see him as a miser, holding on tightly to his money, like King Midas, who was given the magical power that whatever he touched turned to gold, only to have it destroy everything he truly cherished. The figure here seems to cling to his pentacles/coins, as if someone from the city might sneak up and take them; be careful if this card appears with the Seven of Swords.

On the other hand, there are no masses of wealth piled around him. If we think of structure, we might say that he uses his possessions, and maybe work, to give his life some form. Primarily, the four pentacles separate him from the world. He can't touch the ground because of the ones under his feet. The one above him blocks the top of his head (the "crown") from spiritual energy, while the one he holds closes off his heart, lungs, and solar plexus. But we can never really close ourselves off from life, for what about his back?

· · · · · · ·

DIVINATORY MEANINGS:

Holding on tightly to what you have. Using material possessions to structure your life or to close yourself off emotionally from others. Tension as a result of miserliness.

REVERSED:

Letting go of possessions, usually to open up to others or new experiences. Lack of structure in daily life. Possibly a warning to guard what matters most to you.

Five of Pentacles

ELEMENT:
earth

THEME:
difficulties

The theme of difficulties in the element of Earth gives us one of the Tarot's grimmest pictures. A barefoot woman and a bandaged man on crutches, both of them in tatters, make their way through a snowstorm past what seems to be a church with a stained glass window. Churches are supposed to be places of sanctuary for the poor and sick, yet no door appears in the picture.

Some people see the scene as a criticism of the rich, while others focus psychologically on the people themselves, suggesting they have become so identified with their suffering they do not even notice the possibility of shelter. But look closely at the man. Do you see the bell hanging from his neck? In the Middle Ages, people who suffered from Hansen's disease (leprosy) were forced to wear such bells so people fearful of infection could keep away from them. In other words, the people are true outcasts, rejected by society.

But they have each other. No third figure looms above them to define or control their loyalty and mutual help. This card sometimes defines relationships of people united in suffering.

The five pentacles actually form the top half of the Tree of Life. Five is half of ten, where we see the whole Tree, so it makes sense. But without the bottom half, the above can get dangerously disconnected from below.

· · · · · ·

DIVINATORY MEANINGS:

Hardship, either economic or physical, but also loyalty and mutual help. People can become overidentified with their pain and not see other possibilities. Possibly people who live outside society's rules and structures.

REVERSED:

Relief from suffering. Recovery. Possibly aid from others or society. With the card upside down, the window seems to turn into a door. Better times may cause strain in a relationship.

Six of Pentacles

ELEMENT:
earth

THEME:
unequal relationship, generosity

The twin themes of generosity and unequal relationships seem to find their perfect expression in this image
of charity. A man whom Waite describes as "in the guise of
a merchant" gives coins to a beggar while another waits his

turn. Some see the two as the suffering pair of the Five who've found a benefactor, a kind of happy ending.

This is, in fact, one of the most layered and suggestive images in the Minor Arcana. Should the people really have to get on their knees and beg? Notice how carefully he measures out the coins, as if only giving what he knows he can afford. Is this really an image of generosity?

And notice that curious phrase "in the guise of a merchant," and also the balanced scales in his left hand, a reminder of the Major Arcana card Justice. Tarotist Edith Katz once interpreted "guise" as *disguise* and spoke of him as Justice acting in the world through human agents.

Maybe sometimes we *do* need to get on our knees and ask for help, either from friends or family or life itself, and without that willingness nothing can happen. The action needed might not be literal asking but rather the willingness to take the first steps or to allow others to help you—what I call putting yourself in a position to receive. And maybe sometimes we get just what we need at that moment and nothing more.

· · · · · ·

DIVINATORY MEANINGS:

Charity; help to people who need it. This could be emotional or practical help as well as money. Willingness to ask for help or to take actions that allow help to come to you.

REVERSED:

Helping yourself instead of asking for charity. Alternatively, generosity that's not measured out or limited. People helping each other in an equal relationship.

Seven of Pentacles

ELEMENT:

earth

THEME:

action

On the surface a very simple image, this is one of those cards where the interpretation can depend on how we see the figure in the picture. Is he satisfied? Frustrated? Taking a well-earned rest? Anxious about all the work he still needs to do? Part of what makes the Rider deck so endlessly open is just this ambiguity in Smith's images. So don't be afraid to ask the querent what she or he sees in the scene, and especially the attitude of the man looking at the pentacles on the bush.

Pentacles signify the grounding of Earth, and so the theme of action gives way to rest (compare the Knight of Pentacles, the only knight whose horse doesn't move). Or maybe it's not rest so much as it's *contemplating* action, especially work, either already finished or still to come. You might get this card when you're in between projects or assignments at your job.

He leans on what seems to be a garden tool of some kind, a hoe or a shovel half buried in the dirt. This suggests someone who has made his work central to his life. We might compare him to the Hermit, who leans on his staff of wisdom, or to the figure in the Eight of Cups, who uses a similar stick to walk away from his life in search of something higher. The man here seems content to stay and do his work—or maybe he secretly longs to leave. It all depends on how we look at him.

· · · · · · ·

DIVINATORY MEANINGS:

Rest from work; perhaps the contemplation of what comes next. Satisfaction? Frustration? Anxiety? Peace? All these readings are possible, depending on how people see the image.

REVERSED:

Work resumed. The next stage or a new project. Possibly a move to leave a project or a job and seek something else, depending on the question and the other cards.

Eight of Pentacles

ELEMENT:
earth

THEME:
movement

A young man with curly red hair and red tights, wearing what appears to be a stonecutter's apron, sits at a bench calmly chiseling pentacles on disks one after another, it seems. If you look closely at the ones hanging on the wall, you will notice they are each slightly different from the others. We might see this as the sign of a craftsman (as opposed to a machine) or perhaps of an apprentice learning his trade. We might compare him to the master sculptor of the Three of Pentacles. Either way, the theme of movement has become grounded in work. That is, each new pentacle moves him further, not to an end goal (there's no sense of a quota here, or the impatience some see in the Seven) but just in the satisfaction of what he does.

A city appears in the distance, with a road that seems to run from the city gate to the carver's workshop. But no one is there beside him, nor does he appear concerned over whether his pentacles will sell. He seems content just to keep doing what he does.

The eighth position on the Tree of Life is sometimes linked to Mercury, the god of intellect. Mercury is swift and changeable, but in the realm of Pentacles the mind becomes steady, focused, and dedicated to its work.

· · · · · ·

DIVINATORY MEANINGS:

Stability, especially in a work situation. Satisfaction, dedication. Slow, steady progress. The opportunity to work or do some other activity that you enjoy without having to worry about the result.

REVERSED:

Frustration or dissatisfaction with a situation. Possible need to make long-range plans. Moving to a higher level in some important aspect of life—this could apply to relationships or family as well as work.

Nine of Pentacles

ELEMENT:
earth

THEME:
intensity, high degree

The suit of Pentacles outlines a story of success, collapse, and recovery. The early success of the Ace to Four seems to collapse in the Five. Help comes in the Six, and in the Seven we contemplate the result of hard work or maybe all that needs to be done. The Eight shows dedication, and now the Nine gives us the sense of satisfaction from having made something of our lives. This is the intensity of Pentacles, the result of all that effort. The excess of Ten will call values into question, but here we see satisfaction.

She wears a robe decorated with simple flowers that also form the woman symbol of the planet Venus, ruler of love. Even though she stands alone, there is love in the way her hand rests on the pentacle and in the gentle tilt of her head as she looks at her falcon. Grapes grow on the vines, a symbol of abundance and happiness. A snail, symbol of a fertile life, but also stability and security, moves across the bottom of the picture.

The trained falcon, hooded so it won't fly away, symbolizes discipline—not the kind where you grit your teeth and force yourself to do something but rather the willingness to completely apply yourself with training and dedication. She stands alone; maybe she has had to make sacrifices, including relationships. Her number, nine, recalls the Hermit. But she seems to love her life and all that her efforts have created.

· · · · · ·

DIVINATORY MEANINGS:

*Self-discipline, achievement. Satisfaction
with what you have done in your life or with a
career. Maybe the completion of a project.*

REVERSED:

*Lack of discipline, possibly even low regard for yourself.
More likely choosing spontaneity over long-range goals
or taking a break from work to enjoy time with others.*

Ten of Pentacles

ELEMENT:

earth

THEME:

excess

A family stands inside an archway that appears to show a town or a compound of buildings. Everything is orderly inside the arch but somehow stiff as well, especially if we compare these people to the joyous celebrating family of the Ten of Cups. The woman looks over her shoulder at the man, who stares at the buildings. His left hand holds a black pole with a white crystal at the end, a hint of the Chariot or even the Magician. On the right, a child clings to the woman and to the tail of a dog, as if timid to stand on his own.

Meanwhile, just outside the arch, a mysterious white-haired man sits, seen by no one but the two dogs. He wears a patchwork robe full of symbols, as if he carries the mysteries of existence on his back. An excess of Pentacles can mean wealth and security but somehow at the price of real emotional connection between people, and maybe the loss of a sense of the world's wonder.

Throughout the deck we've seen cards whose imagery hinted at the Tree of Life. Parts of it appeared behind the High Priestess, and we saw the top half in the Five of Pentacles. But this is the only card where we see the complete Tree in its proper form, yet it remains separate from the rest of the picture. Compare the Nine, where she touches one of the pentacles, or the Eight, where he actually creates them. Once more, we see a separation between material wealth and the spiritual truth that underlies it.

· · · · · ·

DIVINATORY MEANINGS:

Wealth, security, but possibly a life that seems too dull or narrow. The querent may be missing something important. A fortunetelling tradition sees this card as an inheritance.

REVERSED:

Discovery of deeper meanings in life or even of a wider reality. A family communicates more. Giving up security for adventure and a sense of risk. Possibly problems or delays around an inheritance.

A READING FOR
The Suit of Pentacles

1

4   5

2 3

1. What is my true work?

2. What helps me do it?

3. What holds me back?

4. What do I need to do for my work overall?

5. What action do I need to take right now?

The
Court Cards

The number 4 structures our lives. We have four limbs, two arms and two legs. Our bodies create four directions: front, behind, right, and left. Because Earth spins on an axis, our planet contains a North and a South Pole. Draw a line at right angles to this axis and you get east and west, or just stand facing due north and stretch your arms out: north before you, south behind you, east to the right, and west to the left. There are four special days in the year, two equinoxes and two solstices, and thus four seasons.

Four suits. Four elements. And now we have four court cards in each of the four suits—a page, a knight, a queen, and a king. It's worth remembering that in most sets of playing cards there are only three courts—a jack (page), queen, and king. We can imagine that when people created the earliest card decks, just the suits without the Major Arcana "triumphs," the knights had ridden off somewhere and were not available. When people created the Tarot, however, they wanted the deck to be complete, and so the knights "returned" from their quests and joined the page, the queen, and the king. After all, this is what knights do: they ride off; they go on quests, or missions; they rescue princesses and/or kill dragons. And then they return.

One way to see the court cards is as families: the king and the queen as the parents, the knight and the page as the older and younger children. As we saw with the numbered cards, each position—that is, the page, knight, queen, or king—carries its own quality, and so does each suit, so that Page of Wands, say, combines the qualities of pages and of Wands. Pages are young, and Wands are Fire, so we get Young Fire, untried but eager.

The Hermetic Order of the Golden Dawn formalized this in a very direct way. Since the four suits each belonged to an element, why not the four court positions? In their method, Fire, Water, Air, and Earth belong to king, queen, knight, and page (they actually changed the names, but these are the equivalents with the traditional names). Since Fire, Water, Air, and Earth also belong to Wands, Cups, Swords, and Pentacles, we get two elements for each card.

	Fire WANDS	*Water* CUPS	*Air* SWORDS	*Earth* PENTACLES
Fire KING				
Water QUEEN				
Air KNIGHT				
Earth PAGE				

To find the elemental quality of any card, literally translate its name. For example, the Knight of Cups. Knights are Air, and Cups are Water, so the Knight of Cups becomes Air of Water. Queen of Pentacles. Queens are Water, Pentacles are Earth; thus we get Water of Earth.

In each suit, one card becomes a perfect match. King of Wands is Fire of Fire; Queen of Cups, Water of Water; Knight of Swords, Air of Air; and Page of Pentacles, Earth of Earth. We will list these titles at the head of each card. As with any list of this kind, some may seem more directly meaningful than others. Tarot card reading always remains an art more than a science, with any system a spur to meaning rather than a fixed rule of what something *has* to mean.

We also can look at the court cards in less schematic ways. As well as seeing them as families, we might consider them as stages of development. The pages are beginnings. We often think of them as students learning the quality of their suit. The fiery Page of Wands is eager, excited, ready to enter the world. By contrast, the watery Page of Cups is contemplative, fascinated, quiet. One hallmark of the pages is that they do not carry a great deal of responsibility; they simply experience.

The knights represent the next stage, one of adventure and dedication. Knights are idealistic, perhaps best characterized by the courageous Knight of Swords charging into battle. The knights have more responsibility than the pages. Yes, they get to ride off and have adventures, but we expect them to slay the dragon or find the treasure and then come back.

The queens and kings together form the mature embodiment of the suit. I think of the queens as masters of the element. They understand it and give themselves to it at the highest level. The Queen of Swords points her blade straight up (as with Justice and the Ace) for absolute commitment to truth. The Queen of Wands, in the happier element of Fire, loves life. She sits with her legs apart, holding up her bright sunflower, and as if in return for her positive nature, a black cat has come to protect her.

The kings, on the other hand, carry more responsibility, for in the old medieval system it was the kings who had to make the decisions, hear petitions, and lead the nation. The queens represent mastery; the kings, authority. Of the four, the one most comfortable with this role is the King of Swords, for the suit of mind gives itself to decisions and commands. He is the only court card to look directly at us.

By contrast, some roles go against the element. For example, consider how the King of Wands sits on the edge of his throne. Fire is adventurous, it does not like to be contained, and so the king may look as if he longs for the days when he was just a knight and could ride off on his horse.

This probably is a place to remember a basic rule of Tarot reading: kings do not have to signify men, or queens women. We tend to think of them that way first, but we probably all know women who take commanding, kinglike roles, or men who go deeply into an energy in the manner of a queen. The same openness goes for pages and knights.

As an exercise once, I laid out all the court cards and decided to see if I could give each one a one- or two-word theme, just to see if I could define what makes them unique. It turned out to be much easier than I thought. *Adventure* for the Knight of Wands, for example, versus *courage* for the Knight of Swords. I will list my choices at the head of each court card, but try it yourself. After you've gotten to know the court cards—after you've read about them here or in other books, but especially after they've come up in readings, for yourself or others—just set them all out on the table. Look at each one in turn—at his or her posture and surroundings, at how they relate to their suit emblem—and then see if you can find your own keywords for each of them.

So far, we have looked at the court cards in terms of their qualities, their energy and function. But there is a more traditional way to see them, and that is as actual people. If a woman asks about her marriage, the king might signify her husband, a knight might indicate a lover, a page her child, and a queen herself or maybe another woman. In work situations, the kings can indicate bosses. But how do we know just who a particular court card is supposed to represent?

I prefer to try to identify them by their qualities and energy, and sometimes just by my intuition. However, we also can look at traditional methods of identification based on age and hair and skin color. I have adapted Waite's designations slightly to come up with the following: pages signify children or students of either gender; knights, adults of either gender in their twenties or thirties, especially unmarried; queens, mature women; and kings, mature men. Wands have light hair and blue eyes; Cups, light brown hair and gray or hazel eyes; Swords, dark brown hair and brown eyes; and Pentacles, black hair and black eyes. Despite the fact that I find this approach limited, I have listed these qualities for each card as well.

Finally, we do not have to assume one court card per person. Two queens, for example, might indicate a shift in someone's attitude or experience. If the first card in, say, the Celtic

Cross is the Queen of Swords, but then Near Future turns up the Queen of Pentacles, this might show a lightening of the querent's mind. She might turn from sorrow at some loss to an appreciation of nature.

Because the court cards may signify an actual person, and because the figures don't *do* very much—compare, say, the Knight of Pentacles with the Six of Swords—many people find them among the hardest to interpret. As with everything else, the more you read the cards, the more comfortable you will become when court cards turn up in a spread. And remember, we don't need to live up to the clichéd image of the mystical Tarot reader who knows all, sees all, and tells all (so long as you cross her palm with silver). Sometimes it might work just to ask the querent, "Look closely at this King of Cups. Does he remind you of anybody? Can you see yourself in this picture?"

· · · · · ·

SPECIAL NOTE:

The theme words and the divinatory meanings for the court cards are similar in places to those in my book Tarot Wisdom. *They come from many years of both reading and studying the cards. The descriptions, however, are freshly done for this book.*

Wands

ELEMENT:

fire

ELEMENTAL COMBINATION:

earth of fire

PHYSICAL QUALITY:

a child or young person with light hair and blue eyes

THEME:

eagerness

Oone of Smith's signature androgynous figures, the Page appears as a pretty young man, richly dressed with a decorated tunic, a flowing yellow cape, and a jaunty hat with a red feather that may remind us of the Fool or the Sun child. Standing strong and upright, with his head tilted back and his stick gripped firmly, he seems confident, ready to commit himself to something. As the youngest figure in the court of Wands, we can see him as eager, excited, a card of beginnings. I see the Page of Wands as the first of the court cards (from my developmental approach, the page is the first of each suit, and Wands is the first suit), so everything becomes new and fresh. Like the Knight and Queen he stands in a desert, before either sand dunes or pyramids. Fire always runs the danger of burning out its environment.

Notice the salamanders on his tunic. With most, the tail does not reach the mouth—a symbol of things unfinished (compare the Knight and the King). The future lies before him.

A Tarot tradition calls the pages messengers. What might the message of Fire be? Maybe to enjoy life, to take chances, to begin something. Some people see this card as a faithful lover.

· · · · · ·

DIVINATORY MEANINGS:

Freshness, enthusiasm, a willingness to begin something.

Someone young and energetic. Exciting news.

Possibly a faithful lover or a declaration of love.

REVERSED:

Uncertainly, hesitancy, caution (especially

with the Fool reversed). It may be an unfaithful

lover, especially with the Seven of Swords.

KNIGHT of WANDS.

ELEMENT:

fire

ELEMENTAL COMBINATION:

air of fire

PHYSICAL QUALITY:

an adult, twenties or thirties, with light hair and blue eyes

THEME:

adventure

The basic mission of a knight is simple. He rides out on a quest, he does heroic deeds, and then he comes back, bringing something special from his victories.

With the Knight of Wands, the quest becomes primarily adventure. He is dashing, intense, energetic. He gets annoyed, frustrated, or impatient with whatever is dull and repetitious, but at the same time he remains heroic, idealistic.

The horse rears up as if he, too, can hardly contain himself. Interestingly, he's not actually going anywhere, but unlike the stolid black horse of the Knight of Pentacles, this golden horse looks about to gallop off—somewhere—as soon as his hooves touch the ground. The Knight of Wands can be just that sort of individual idealist, not wanting to belong to any group but eager to right wrongs—as long as it's not boring.

We see salamanders—fire lizards—on his tunic, similar to the Page and King. With most of them, the tail does not reach the mouth—a symbol of things unfinished. He has much to experience before he can think of settling down.

* * * * * *

DIVINATORY MEANINGS:

Adventure, daring. Someone energetic and forceful. As a person, he can be very charming and confident. This can be a card of travel.

REVERSED:

Possible delays and interruptions. Overconfidence, as if the Knight might have fallen off his horse because he was just not ready for everything he was trying to do.

QUEEN of WANDS.

ELEMENT:
fire

ELEMENTAL COMBINATION:
water of fire

PHYSICAL QUALITY:
an older woman with light hair and blue eyes

THEME:
love of life

She sits on a throne in the desert, with carved lions on either side and lions rampant painted on the back. The Golden Dawn identified her with Leo, sign of the lion, and the fixed sign of summer. In fact, sunflowers adorn her throne, and she holds a living sunflower in her left hand, along with the wand in her right. We might think of the radiant Sun card, where a line of sunflowers grows behind the child. Her crown appears covered in flowers, compared to the King's fiery gold. She has watered the desert—brought feeling to the aggressiveness of Fire.

Along with the carved lions we see a living feline, a black cat, like a witch's familiar (Wiccans often identify with this card), as if nature has sent her a guardian.

This queen is confident, strong, happy. The essential quality of the queen is mastery, and she is the master of Fire, the feminine part of complete confidence. Wands are sexual energy, and in the Rider she is famously the most sexual of the queens, for she sits with her legs apart.

Her calm confidence makes her a good person to have around in a crisis. However, we can't push her too far. Her Leo confidence and desire for happiness can get annoyed if people seem weak or overly emotional.

. . . . . .

DIVINATORY MEANINGS:

She is confident, life-giving, and generous but sometimes
fierce. She can be passionate sexually but impatient
with a partner who shows weakness or hesitation. A
love of life, possibly a time of ease and enjoyment.

REVERSED:

Generous and good in a crisis, the Queen can become impatient with situations that go on too long. She needs to be around people and in situations that embrace life, and she can have trouble understanding limitations.

KING of WANDS

ELEMENT:
fire

ELEMENTAL COMBINATION:
fire of fire

PHYSICAL QUALITY:
an older man with light hair and blue eyes

THEME:
confidence (arrogance)

He sits strongly on his throne, wearing a red robe and a red helmet under his gold crown shaped like flames. His stern expression and the way his left hand appears half clenched in a fist suggest impatience. Lions and salamanders appear on the back of his throne, with more salamanders covering the outside of his cloak. They all form circles with their tales in their mouths, symbolic of completion and maturity (compare the Page and the Knight). A small black salamander appears on the platform of his throne.

Queens master their element, but kings are required to rule, to make decisions. This King in the element of Fire can be confident to the point of arrogant, not so much from nastiness as simply a difficulty understanding people who are hesitant or doubtful.

The role of king requires him to sit on his throne and be available for governing, for people seeking his help (in modern life, it can mean just having to go to work each day), and this can be a problem. Fire wants to move—to seek freedom and reject whatever would hold it down. Notice he seems to sit upright rather then lean back on his throne, as if he fantasizes about being a knight and riding off to look for dragons to kill or maidens to rescue. Or he might envy the Queen, who seems (to him) to enjoy her good life without responsibilities.

. . . . . .

DIVINATORY MEANINGS:

*An older man (or possibly a woman), very strong and
confident. He may be impatient with those who act or
think too slowly and who cannot stand up to his tendency
to take charge. He has no guile, however, or ill will, just
a powerful energy. A confident, demanding boss.*

REVERSED:

*Tested or in any way confined, he may react angrily.
His desire for adventure may cause him to give up
responsibility or resent what he does for others.*

Cups

PAGE of CUPS.

ELEMENT:
water

ELEMENTAL COMBINATION:
earth of water

PHYSICAL QUALITY:
*a child or young person with light brown hair
and gray or hazel eyes*

THEME:
imagination

Graceful and relaxed, with perhaps an amused or fascinated expression, he watches as a fish rises from the cup (or just rests on the edge). Like the Pages of Cups and Pentacles, he wears beautiful clothes—a flowing hat, a tunic decorated with lotus flowers. The lotus grows in water, with long stems to allow the graceful flower to emerge into the sun; thus it symbolizes consciousness emerging from the primal sea of being. As far back as the early nineteenth century, this card has meant "meditation…contemplation" (from the French diviner Etteila). In Egyptian myth the sun god is born in a lotus, while in India the lotus blossom can represent the divine feminine.

Behind the Page we see the simplest possible drawing of waves. Compare it to the energetic sea of the King. For the Page (who is without responsibilities), emotion and imagination remain simple, something to look at the way he looks at the fish.

Do the Page and the fish talk to each other? They may remind us of fairy tales of miraculous talking animals that have the power to grant wishes. Often in the stories greed or selfishness create disastrous outcomes. The Page of Cups, however, shows no desire, only delight. If all the Cups are messengers, what message does he bring us? Maybe just to stay silent, to observe the flowing waters, and enjoy what emerges from our own imagination.

· · · · · ·

DIVINATORY MEANINGS:

Quiet, meditation. An interest in spiritual or imaginative subjects without any need to do anything with them. Someone who loves beautiful things. Messages from the subconscious, including psychic information.

REVERSED:

Someone troubled by things that come from the imagination or the subconscious. Pressure and responsibility to act or make decisions.

KNIGHT of CUPS.

ELEMENT:
water

ELEMENTAL COMBINATION:
air of water

PHYSICAL QUALITY:
*an adult, twenties or thirties, with light brown hair
and gray or hazel eyes*

THEME:
dreams, introspection

His gray horse moves slowly, with head bowed, the opposite of the rearing Wands horse or the galloping Swords but not as stolid as Pentacles. Fish adorn his tunic for the Water part of his identity, while feathers appear on his helmet and stirrups for Air; Air of Water. He holds the cup out as if to offer it, but he also stares at it, perhaps uncertain that he wants to let it go.

This card is an interesting one to show up in relationship readings. Knights are figures of romance. In the courtly love tradition, the knight dedicates his strength selflessly to the service and adoration of the lady. And Cups is a romantic suit. But Cups are also dreamy—they can turn inwards, drawn by fantasies or their own emotions. This Knight may be drawn to love and yet desire to pursue his own inner life. If he shows up in a reading next to the Hermit, the inward quality becomes stronger. Next to the Lovers or the Two of Cups, the romantic side becomes stronger.

When this card comes up, we might ask what he is questing for on his slow-moving horse. Does the cup guide him? Is that why he stares at it? Or is the cup his prize, and his horse moves so slowly because he's not sure he wants to give it up? Ask yourself (or the querent) what the cup might represent to you; what do you see in it?

· · · · · ·

DIVINATORY MEANINGS:

Someone romantic, dreamy, caught up in fantasies, and slow moving. He may be a devoted lover but also someone just fascinated by love itself and his own fantasies.

REVERSED:

*Something may stir him to action. Love may
rouse him from self-absorption.*

QUEEN of CUPS.

ELEMENT:
water

ELEMENTAL COMBINATION:
water of water

PHYSICAL QUALITY:
*an older woman with light brown hair
and gray or hazel eyes*

THEME:
dedication

She sits on a throne adorned with carvings of what look like mermaid cherubs, with a scallop shell behind her head. The throne rests on dry land; compare this to the King's, which floats on the sea. At the same time, river water swirls all around her and even seems to merge into her dress, so that we can say she blends intense feeling with action and a connection to practical reality.

Water of Water. As one of the four pure elemental cards, the Queen of Cups carries a special power, intense and dedicated to the highest quality of her suit: selfless love. Waite says of her "she sees but she also acts, and her activity feeds her dream." She stares at her elaborate cup, which stands out in the deck as unique—the only one decorated and the only one covered. Like the Ace of Cups, it carries more obvious spiritual meanings than most Minor cards. Some compare it to the vessel that holds the sacred wafers that turn into the body of Christ in the Catholic Mass. The winged figures on either side suggest the two seraphim who were said to guard the Ark of the Covenant at the center of the temple in ancient Israel.

The Ark was the dwelling place of the Shekhinah, the female presence of the Divine. The Queen of Cups can be invoked magically for healing or love. Set her on an altar, with flowers around her and an elegant bowl of water in front of her.

- - - - - - -

DIVINATORY MEANINGS:

Intensity, love. The ability to feel and also act. She may represent a creative artist or creativity itself. She also can indicate love, either romantic love or love of family. Healing or protection in some difficult situation.

REVERSED:

The unity of vision and action can weaken so that she either gets lost in her inner worlds or acts without genuine emotion. Possible emotional strains in a family.

KING *of* CUPS.

ELEMENT:

water

ELEMENTAL COMBINATION:

fire of water

PHYSICAL QUALITY:

an older man with light brown hair and gray or blue eyes

THEME:

channeled creativity

Ilf you set the Queen and King of Cups next to each other, in the standard order of the Queen on the left, you will notice that this married couple look away from each other.

They seem to go their separate ways, maybe even have other lovers. Think of their elemental qualities. Being Water of Water, the Queen doesn't really need a partner to express her love and devotion; she might do it through family or service. The King's Fire of Water puts him in an interesting situation. The Water is emotion or creative impulse, but Fire pushes him to action in the world beyond the Cups' realm of the heart. As King, he needs to seek success and accomplishment to make his mark and be responsible.

The King of Cups may be a very creative, sensitive person, a dreamer like the Knight, who has channeled all that sensitivity into his business or professional life—say, a poet who becomes a successful lawyer.

His throne floats on the vibrant sea, yet the water doesn't touch his feet, unlike the Queen, whose throne rests on dry land, yet the river seems to flow into her dress. The King of Cups may indicate someone with deep levels of feeling who does not show this side to others lest it rise up and flood him.

- - - - - -

DIVINATORY MEANINGS:

Someone successful, maybe with deep emotions or creative impulses that he tends to hide. This may be a card of achievement in the arts or in professions of channeled creativity such as law or business consulting. Possibly someone with a drinking problem who manages to cover it up (but only when other cards hint at this).

REVERSED:

The emotions may come out more, especially if other cards indicate a crisis. Anger or tears may reveal long-hidden feelings. There may be blocked creativity or frustration.

Swords

PAGE of SWORDS.

ELEMENT:
air

ELEMENTAL COMBINATION:
earth of air

PHYSICAL QUALITY:
a young person with dark brown hair and brown eyes

THEME:
caution, wariness

We see the Page on a windy hilltop among the clouds. If he is Earth of Air, the Air part is stronger than the Earth. He looks back over his shoulder, holding his sword aloft. He is the most masculine of the pages, his tunic undecorated, without a hat or hood. But what do we make of the black form that streams behind his head? A ribbon? An extension of cloud? An energy form? Notice that it resembles the black tree blowing in the wind at the bottom left. As light as the Page seems, there is a quality of darkness in him, as if he has witnessed painful things.

The pages represent students or beginners who do not need to take action but simply study or appreciate their element. The Page of Swords is lighter than the other Swords court cards—not ferocious like the Knight or grim like the Queen or serious as the King. At the same time, he appears wary as he holds the heavy sword with both hands and looks backwards (like so many of the figures in the Swords suit, who look back or cover their faces or are blindfolded). He does not ride directly into battle, like the Knight, but looks cautious, as if he might have to defend himself at any moment. An interesting fortunetelling tradition describes him as a spy. What might that mean in a reading?

• • • • • •

DIVINATORY MEANINGS:

Caution, wariness. Looking backward, perhaps nervously.
Tension before a fight. Someone who spies or investigates.

REVERSED:

Learning to relax, to trust people. Alternatively, the exact opposite: becoming more anxious, more aggressive. Other cards can suggest which way it goes.

KNIGHT of SWORDS.

ELEMENT:

air

ELEMENTAL COMBINATION:

air of air

PHYSICAL QUALITY:

*an adult, twenties or thirties, with
dark brown hair and brown eyes*

THEME:

courage

He is the most "knightly" of the four knights, riding head-long into battle, his sword held high, his red cape and feathers streaming behind him. Butterflies and birds, the animals of Air, adorn the horse, but if his armor carries decorations, his aggressive, bent-over posture conceals them.

In the elemental combinations, he is perfect Air. We might think of him as dwelling in the high places of the mind, moving swiftly as only Air can—quick-thinking, lofty, principled, brilliant.

Despite his strong elemental power, the Knight of Swords' main attribute is courage. Waite identified him with Sir Galahad, the great champion from the Grail stories who is courageous and idealistic but also remote. The Knight of Swords rides directly into a storm—the trees bend toward him, and even the horse seems to look back nervously, as if to say, "Are you sure we should do this?" The Knight, however, does not recognize such caution.

The Knight of Swords charges courageously forward, but he needs to make sure he serves some higher purpose than just the love of battle. Ultimately the sword he holds is the sword of Justice or the Ace's emblem of truth.

· · · · · ·

DIVINATORY MEANINGS:

Courage, swiftness, daring. Battle can be suggested,
and whoever takes up this sword needs to make sure
he or she fights for justice. The intellect at a pure level
(Air of Air). Brilliant ideas. A fast-moving mind.

REVERSED:

The danger of fighting for its own sake, for the thrill of battle. With all the Swords court cards, the reversed can tend toward corruption, and the Knight can become aggressive, overbearing. More simply, he can take on a wild or reckless quality.

ELEMENT:
air

ELEMENTAL COMBINATION:
water of air

PHYSICAL QUALITY:
an older woman with dark brown hair and brown eyes

THEME:
wisdom, sorrow

She sits on a simple but elegant throne adorned with butter-flies and the winged head of a cherub. We might recall the winged lion's head from the Two of Cups; however, unlike the couple in that card, the Queen is alone.

Many people see her as a figure of sorrow, even a widow. In fact, the tassel hanging from her left hand may represent a Victorian mark of widowhood, though some see her as the woman from the Eight of Swords, who has cut herself free and wears the cord as a reminder of her dark time. Butterflies form her crown, symbolic of the transformation of the soul from sorrow or pain to spiritual truth through the purity of mind. The Greek word *psyche*, which today means the mind, originally meant both butterfly and soul, for the butterfly changes, miraculously, from a sluggish creature of the dirt to a winged spirit of beauty.

She scowls, or so most people would read her expression. She is not happy—she may have seen a good deal of sorrow or pain in her life—but her head rises above the clouds, a symbol of her purity, her refusal to look away or deny her truth. And she holds up an open hand, welcoming life and spirit and also offering what she has learned, holding nothing back. She does not tilt the sword as if ready to fight but holds it straight up, like the swords on Justice and the Ace. She knows that with-out her commitment to truth, she has nothing. One bird flies above her, a further image of her pure mind.

· · · · · · ·

DIVINATORY MEANINGS:

Possibly sorrow, even widowhood or some other difficulty that can leave someone alone yet wise. Commitment to truth both in thought and speech, though her speech can be harsh, as she refuses to sugarcoat her honesty. Possibly an intellectual, a writer.

REVERSED:

As with the other Swords court cards, reversed can slide toward corruption—that powerful mind and personality turned more toward manipulation and control. Another (happier) interpretation would see her as leaving her high, lonely place and becoming more involved in life, possibly in a relationship.

KING of SWORDS.

ELEMENT:

air

ELEMENTAL COMBINATION:

fire of air

PHYSICAL QUALITY:

an older man with dark brown hair and brown eyes

THEME:

authority

L ooking oddly like Lawrence of Arabia, he sits in a high place among the clouds. His throne rises behind him like a stone pillar, carved with butterflies and winged spirits known as sylphs, the elemental creature of Air. Like Justice, whom he resembles, he looks directly at us, the only court card of the sixteen to do so. Authority and responsibility are the primary qualities of the kings, and the thoughtful King of Swords seems more suited to that role than any other. The Wands king looks like he wants to abdicate, the Cups like he must suppress his Water feelings, while the Pentacles king focuses primarily on his wealth. The King of Swords looks out at us with a sense of command.

At the same time, the need to make decisions and take action means that he cannot maintain the sense of purity found in the detached Queen. Her sword points straight up (like Justice and the Ace); his tilts to the side. Where one bird appears in the Queen's card, two fly behind the King, symbolic of the choices he must make. Perhaps more than any other king, he thinks constantly of the consequences of his decisions.

In work or career readings, all the Kings may indicate bosses. The King of Swords will be smarter than everyone else and mindful of his responsibilities.

• • • • • •

DIVINATORY MEANINGS:

Someone in a position of authority who is comfortable making decisions and being in command. As well as a person, the King of Swords can signify the very idea of a wise decision, especially for the common good.

REVERSED:

A powerful mind and personality serving itself rather than society. Possibly a corrupt boss or other authority figure. More benignly, putting off an important decision.

Pentacles

PAGE of PENTACLES.

ELEMENT:

earth

ELEMENTAL COMBINATION:

earth of earth

PHYSICAL QUALITY:

*a young person with very dark brown or black hair
and black eyes*

THEME:

study

This is the unified elemental card in the suit, Earth of Earth. We might expect to see someone grounded, aware of physical things, physically heavy. Instead we see someone graceful, aware of nothing at all but his pentacle gently held up before him. He appears to be walking slowly as he stares, fascinated, at the magic star in its golden circle. All the pages can signify students, but Pentacles seems the very model of a dedicated scholar, devoted to his studies just for the love of learning.

If pages are messengers, what message would he bring us? Maybe he would tell us what he sees in that lightly held pentacle. Maybe he is a diviner staring into his crystal ball. Or, remembering that pentacles are signs of magic, he might be a beginner in occult studies who follows the wonder of the pentacle. His posture and openness may remind us of the Fool, ready to enter a new world. Unlike the Fool, he moves slowly, led by his bright pentacle to wherever it will take him.

· · · · · ·

DIVINATORY MEANINGS:

A student or beginner in something—magic or any other area of learning. Fascination with something without the need to do anything except follow the wonder of it. Dedication. Tuning out the world around you.

REVERSED:

A student may have trouble with his studies or feel some outside pressure, such as the need to pass exams or think about career. Alternatively, it can mean relaxation after intense study or work.

KNIGHT of PENTACLES.

ELEMENT:
earth

ELEMENTAL COMBINATION:
air of earth

PHYSICAL QUALITY:
*an adult, twenties or thirties, with very dark brown
or black hair and black eyes*

THEME:
work

He sits upright on a large black horse, whose face is decorated with leaves the same as the Knight's helmet. His gloved hand holds out the pentacle as if to present it, while beyond him we see what looks like furrowed fields. Is he their protector, their hero?

As we've noted before, knights go on quests; they slay dragons and rescue maidens. But this Knight doesn't seem to move. The horse stands squarely on the grass. The suit's Earth element grounds the Knight's quality of Air, the swiftness of mind brought down to reality.

The Knight of Pentacles shows us the image of the dedicated worker, not ambitious or given to risk but willing to give all his attention to his duties. While less romantic than Cups, less heroic than Swords, less energetic than Wands, he might be just what we need in certain situations. If you face a challenge at work or some other practical area in life—the plowed fields suggest gardening—where you need to give it your all for a period of time without laziness or distraction or impatience, you might want to invoke the Knight of Pentacles. Whenever you're tempted to check email, take a coffee break, or go lie down for awhile, you can think of the Knight solidly on his horse and stay focused on your task.

· · · · · ·

DIVINATORY MEANINGS:

Hard-working, diligent, devoted to the task at hand, without need for outer rewards or glory. Cautious, not given to wildness or risk. Mind in the service of nature, without ego.

REVERSED:

Too much inertia, possibly allowing others to take advantage of you. Alternatively, finding other interests besides work.

QUEEN of PENTACLES

ELEMENT:

earth

ELEMENTAL COMBINATION:

water of earth

PHYSICAL QUALITY:

*an older woman with very dark brown
or black hair and black eyes*

THEME:

nature

S he sits on a throne in a garden, the stone seat ornately carved with images of fruit (for her love of earth) and goat heads (for her sign of Capricorn). Everything is fruitful, lush. A rabbit, symbol of fertility, appears on the bottom right.

For many people, the Queen of Pentacles reminds us of the Empress, with a deep love of nature, a joy in that lush vegetation that grows all around her. As Water of Earth, she brings passionate love to the living world. She sits in nature, with no buildings in sight, compared to the Pentacles King, whose palace stands behind him. Notice that she shares certain qualities with the Magician. Like him, she wears red over white, and like him, leaves and flowers arch over her, as if to protect her. But she does not reach up toward the heavens to draw Above down into Below; she just holds her magic pentacle before her, perhaps looking into its mysteries.

Waite clearly thought very highly of this Queen, describing her as "summed up in the idea of greatness of soul" and "the serious cast of intelligence; she contemplates her symbol and may see worlds therein." For me, she loves nature, passionately and for its own sake.

● ● ● ● ● ●

DIVINATORY MEANINGS:

A love of nature. Intense involvement with the physical world. Happiness, physical security, possibly wealth.

REVERSED:

The essential connection to nature may be lost or threatened, and she can become irritable, aggressive. She may close herself off from family or friends.

KING of PENTACLES.

ELEMENT:
earth

ELEMENTAL COMBINATION:
fire of earth

PHYSICAL QUALITY:
*older man with very dark brown or
black hair and black eyes*

THEME:
wealth

He sits on a wide throne decorated with bull's heads to symbolize his sign of Taurus. A garden overflows all around him, and his very robe appears hung with clusters of grapes, making him almost a part of the landscape. Behind him rises a castle, or maybe a city. This is the only time we see the actual evidence of a kingdom, for his brothers in the other suits rule over aspects of life, but he is the king of the element of Earth, the "real" world in all its richness.

He is successful, secure, with wealth and possibly honor, and he seems to like it that way as he sits comfortably, almost fondling his pentacle like a child on his knee. Unlike the other crowned figure in this suit, the Four, he does not seem to hoard his wealth but displays it proudly. If you seek to find a benefactor for a project or to win a grant or just to get a raise or promotion, you might visualize the King of Pentacles entering your life. This is also a good card to receive if you are looking for a job, because he can mean a friendly boss.

He represents what we sometimes call "the good life": wealth, comfort, a magnanimous person who appreciates the good things life has given him. At the same time, he may seem more concerned with his own enjoyment than with responsibilities or decisions.

• • • • • •

DIVINATORY MEANINGS:

Wealth, success, comfort, security. He may focus on material things, but more with satisfaction and pride than selfishness or obsession. He can, in fact, be very generous. A good card in any reading that concerns looking for work or material support from someone.

REVERSED:

Worries about money or physical insecurity. Dissatisfaction; a feeling that what you have is not enough. Possibly a turn from material concerns to more abstract or spiritual ideas.

A READING INSPIRED BY
The Court Cards

1	2
3	4
5	6

This spread is inspired by the idea of considering the court cards as distinct families. Though it concerns the courts, it uses the entire deck and is done in the usual manner. I've posed the questions in the present tense, but for people who want to look back at their families when younger, you can do it in the past, changing "Who am I..." to "Who was I..." For simplicity's sake, I have restricted the subjects to self, mother, and father, but of course you could easily add on brothers, sisters, grandparents, etc., depending on your family structure.

1. Who am I in my family?

2. What is my role?

3. Who is my mother?

4. What is her role?

5. Who is my father?

6. What is his role?

Readings

When you strip away all the trappings, reading Tarot cards is simple. The querent—the person who wants to consult the cards—states the issue or question. It can be as general as "I'm concerned about love" or as specific as "I want to know if my marriage is headed for divorce." The reader then chooses a spread—a pattern to lay out the cards. Next, the querent shuffles the deck (facedown so that she or he cannot see the cards) and gives the deck back to the reader, who lays them out according to the spread and says what he or she sees in the cards. The trick, of course, lies in the seeing, but also in the saying—that is, the ability to communicate whatever thoughts or intuitions bubble up when we look at the cards.

It should be pointed out here that if you read for yourself, then the querent and the reader are, in fact, the same person: you. I will write about this process as if the querent and reader are separate people, but you can apply all these methods to reading for yourself. There is a belief among some people that Tarot readers should never read their own cards. Some think it's bad luck, others just that you can't be objective. But if you talk with a group of Tarot readers, you'll find that just about all of them read for themselves. And if you've looked at the spreads in this book inspired by the individual cards or suits, you'll see that most are written to be read for one's self: "What can I learn…"

Are there special rules for shuffling or handling the cards? Yes, many of them. Lots and lots of "rules," but we don't need to obey them. Books and teachers will tell you where to sit, what to say, even how to dress or what to eat or drink before a reading. But you are free to find your own way to that place where you can understand the cards and share that understanding with a querent. Let's look at some of those rules— and the reality.

You don't need to wrap your cards in silk or keep them in a special box. Many experienced readers simply keep their cards in the original cardboard box. Others, however, like the tradition of a beautiful wrapping or container.

Similarly, you do not need to make sure no one else touches your cards. Some readers want to keep their decks "pure," with only their own energy, and so they won't let anyone touch them. I'm actually the opposite; I *want* the querent— the person getting the reading, after all—to shuffle the deck so their energy goes into the cards. If, however, you feel drawn to the idea that only you should handle the deck, go with that intuition. When doing a reading for someone, shuffle the cards yourself, fan them facedown on the table, and ask the person to point to one, then another, until you have the cards for the reading.

And now, let's take a look at one of the strangest ideas you may find floating around on the edges of Tarot—that you should steal, not buy, your Tarot deck. I have no idea where this bizarre notion comes from, but it's certainly not true. I bought my first Tarot deck in 1970 and was thrilled to find it. Strangely, someone did, in fact, steal it from me! I immediately went out and found another. I now have hundreds of Tarot decks and am happy to report that I didn't steal a single one of them.

Another rule you may encounter is the idea that you should *always* include the possibility for reversed cards—or, alternatively, that you should *never* do so. Reversed simply means that the person shuffles them in such a way that some of the cards come out the wrong way around.

In my books about Tarot I have always included reversed meanings, for two reasons. First, Waite included them in his book *The Pictorial Key* one hundred years ago, and who am I to go against Waite? Second, they provide subtle shifts in the cards' possible meanings, and many people like them. However, some never use them, and I often don't myself. If you want to include reversed meanings, ask the querent to shuffle the deck in such a way that some get turned around. On the other hand, if you don't want to use reversals, and a card accidentally comes out that way, don't hesitate to turn it right-side up.

Connected to this question, there is no one correct way to shuffle the cards and no single way to turn them over. Some people love rules, and they will tell you there is only one proper way to mix the deck. The fact is, I have shuffled them a great variety of ways, and they all seem to work. I do, however, ask querents to shuffle them facedown.

People who insist on one correct way to shuffle often also prescribe how to turn them over. Do it however seems right to you, but know that most readers make sure to turn over each card in the same way.

You do not need to place the cards on a "spread cloth"— but they're fun. A spread cloth is a beautiful fabric that covers the table before you begin. It can give the reading more atmosphere as well as separate the table from its everyday "mundane" use. Other things that people do include lighting a candle, setting out some special object, or even saying a short prayer for guidance. None of these are necessary, but they can help you attune to your own intuitive awareness.

Here is another rule that many people insist on, but it can actually block your progress in using the cards: the idea that you should memorize all the meanings before you attempt a reading. I began reading right away, with the cards in one hand and Eden Gray's book of meanings in the other. Some of those readings were the most powerful I've ever done. If you memorize everything ahead of time, you may tend to ignore the pictures and just recite fixed meanings.

Now let's look at a tricky one: should you read for people who are not there and don't know you're doing it? Often this is exactly what querents want from a Tarot reader. "Is my boyfriend cheating on me?" they might ask. Or "What is my daughter up to at college? Is she having sex? Is she using drugs?"

Tarot readers see two problems with this kind of request. First, it's unethical—a kind of spying (though recently I wondered, if you're a private detective who uses Tarot cards, and someone hires you to find out that sort of thing, does that make it okay?). Second, if the boyfriend or daughter is not there to mix the cards, the reading might reflect the *querent's* fears rather than what the other person is doing.

And now the really big question: do you have to be psychic to read Tarot cards? Many people confuse Tarot readers with psychics, so much so that when someone calls me for a reading, I will usually caution them that I don't try to make psychic predictions. Such insights may come up in the reading, but I prefer to look primarily at people's situations and choices, and their emotional and spiritual truths. And I read the cards, not the person.

Of course, psychics do read with Tarot cards. The pictures help trigger responses in whatever part of themselves gives forth psychic messages. Some psychics never bother to learn the cards' deeper symbolism, but a surprising number have steeped themselves in the Tarot's complex traditions.

You can use the Tarot to develop your intuitive abilities. When you read for people, let your mind stay open for flashes or images. Don't try to force them, but let them come, and then be willing to express them. Don't worry about sounding ridiculous or absurd saying something that seemingly comes from nowhere. Recently I've noticed that when Tarot readers trade stories of psychic moments, they often say, "I don't know where that came from" or even "I told her 'I have no idea what this means…'"

The process does not have to be completely mysterious. If you look at the Nine of Swords, which shows a woman crying in bed, and you get a sense of a frightened child, you might say, "Did something scary happen to you when you were little? And did you feel very alone about it?" The important thing about such moments is not to show off your psychic ability but to look at what that experience means. What effect did it have? Why might it be coming up now?

Some predictions may look psychic but simply come from the cards. If a woman is seeking love, and the Knight of Cups appears in the Near Future part of the Celtic Cross, you might say, "Someone is about to enter your life. He will be romantic and dreamy, but he may also be self-involved." If someone asks about a lawsuit and both Justice and the King of Swords come up but are reversed, you might warn the person against a biased judge (this sort of reading is an example of why reversed cards can be helpful).

If you want to make such predictions, you might want to check with the person later, if possible, to see how they turn out. On the other hand, it's important not to get too attached to how "accurate" your readings are. The reading is for the querent, not the reader.

Spreads

The spread is the basic unit of Tarot reading. Even if you just turn over one card with the simplest question, that is a spread. True, some readers will just turn over cards more or less at random until something clicks in them, but for most the spread helps to understand the issues and what the cards have to say about them. There are hundreds, thousands, of spreads, with more invented every day. Go to a Tarot online forum and you will encounter any number of spreads. People have published entire books containing nothing but Tarot spreads, often grouped under various headings such as "Work Spreads" or "Relationship Spreads."

The spreads that follow come from my own forty years of experience. Some are traditional, some I have created or borrowed from friends. As with the spreads for the individual Major Arcana cards, a number have appeared in my book *Tarot Wisdom,* but I have revised them here where it seemed helpful.

The simplest spread would consist of one card, one question: "What do I need to look at right now?" Many people do this on a daily basis as a way to get to know the cards. It can take some of the direness out of reading, since no matter what it is, it's just for that day. If you want to do it as a learning experience, write down what card it is and any interpretation (if nothing comes to you, that's fine), and then before going to sleep, look at the card again and see if it matches some aspect of your day. If you get, say, the Tower, don't immediately assume something awful will happen. It may mean something as simple as your boss getting all worked up about a sudden deadline.

Two-Card Spreads

Two cards sometimes convey a sense of opposition, one side versus another. As a result, many people add a third card to see what can bridge the two. However, there are many two-card spreads.

YOU—SOMEONE ELSE (THIS CAN BE A PARTNER,

A CHILD, A PARENT, A COLLEAGUE, ETC.)

CHOICE ONE—CHOICE TWO

When faced with a clear choice, it's helpful to ask the cards to show us something important about each one. Notice that we are not asking which is better, just what we need to know about each one.

PAST ACTIONS—PRESENT RESULT

This can actually be done several times, looking at different actions. It will still be a two-card reading, just repeated.

Three-Card Spreads

We all come from the mixed genes of a mother and a father, even if we don't know them; thus, three feels natural to us. Some three-card spreads just add one more to the two. For example, Past Actions—Present Result easily becomes:

PAST ACTIONS—PRESENT RESULT—LIKELY FUTURE

This is a variation on the most well-known three-card spread: Past, Present, Future. In that version, however, the past has the quality of fixed fate, and the future a destiny that cannot be changed. Here we emphasize our own actions and what likely will come from them, but it's not an absolute prediction.

Choices

Three-card spreads can help us look at choices. To do this, we first lay a card in the middle for the situation, then set out the choices on either side. Notice that we don't set the cards out 1, 2, 3, but 2, 1, 3. To make this easier to visualize, I will place them on separate lines:

CARD 1

CARD 2   CARD 3

These then represent:

SITUATION

CHOICE A   CHOICE B

This spread is very useful when looking at actual choices. The most common one is between two lovers. Card 1, in the center, would show you something about your feelings right now—what matters to you around relationship. The Devil might emphasize sex; the Ten of Cups, family. This central card will help you look at the choices. Choice A would show you what it might be like with one lover, choice B with the other. Notice that the choice still remains with you; the cards just help you see them better.

You can expand this reading by adding more cards, either for more choices or for the more long-term consequences—results—of each choice.

1: *Situation*

2: *Choice A*   3: *Choice B*

4: *Result of A*   5: *Result of B*

Do/Don't Do Spread

Here is a reading I find very useful, using the same order of placing card 1 in the middle. It comes from Tarotist Zoe Matoff. I often use it as a daily spread.

1: *Situation*

2: *Don't Do*   3: *Do*

Card 1, in the middle, shows us the basic issue. If it's a day spread, it's just what's going on. If I have an actual question, then the first card shows me some important aspect of it.

Card 2, on the left, shows something we should avoid. Often this is something we want to do. For example, when I have a conflict with someone, I always want to call them and try to make it all better. If card 2 was the Three of Cups, it would tell me to avoid such artificial attempts to make the problem go away. Card 3, on the right, shows what would likely help the situation.

I have used this spread for major decisions, for navigating a delicate situation, for tensions in a relationship, for guidance in a creative project—and just to see what the cards want to show me at a particular moment I feel like doing a reading.

Once for my daily spread I got the following cards:

SITUATION: *Tower*

DON'T DO: *Chariot*   DO: *Seven of Swords*

There were no explosive situations in my life at that time, and I really could not see what the Tower might describe. As a result, I forgot about it. Later that day, I took my dog, Wonder, for a walk. Though I live in the country, my house is on a main road, and so I usually drive with her to a quiet place where we don't have to worry about traffic.

Though Wonder is a delight and loves people, she is what's called "dog aggressive," with a tendency to fight other dogs. As a result, I keep her on a leash and try to avoid loose dogs who might come running up to her. That day, we walked down a peaceful road for a ways, but suddenly, just after we'd passed a certain house, two ferocious German shepherds came charging out at us. I had to shout at them at the same time I was restraining my own dog from wanting to take them on, but we managed to get away.

But now I had a dilemma. I couldn't get back to my car to go home without going past that house, and what if they attacked again? It struck me that we should tough it out— just march past them and get it over with. Then suddenly I remembered the reading. The Tower, with its two figures falling headfirst, was the house with the two dogs. My go-ahead idea was the Chariot, strong and willful, but the reading said "don't do" that. Instead, it recommended the softer, even sneaky, approach of the Seven of Swords. So I went far from the house, waited a good while, then walked the dog quietly back to my car without any trouble. I don't know for sure that the more Chariotlike approach would have resulted in disaster, but I'm glad the cards warned me not to do it.

A Three-Card Relationship Spread

Here is a three-card spread for relationships where the final card goes in the middle.

1: *person A's action or attitude*   2: *person B's action or attitude*

3: *the resulting relationship*

You could do this spread with both people present. The reader shuffles the deck (so that neither person determines the energy of the cards), then fans the cards out on the table. Person A chooses a card to represent his or her actions/attitudes. Person B chooses a card for the same question. Then the reader chooses a card on behalf of the relationship.

Spreads with More Cards

Once we go above three cards, the possibilities become endless (or at least up to seventy-eight, but then we could always add more decks). The last time I searched online for "Tarot spreads" (a few years ago), it yielded 101,000 results. I've just tried it again and got 360,000.

Here are a few spreads that I've found useful.

The Doorway Spread

I developed this spread originally for my book *Seeker*, a book aimed at teenagers but one that many adults found very helpful. Instead of emphasizing events, the spread looks at who we are and what our issues are, especially around an important choice. This spread works well for reading your own cards.

Turn over five cards in the following pattern:

1 2

3

4 5

1. What inspires you?

What touches you, what excites you about life, what makes you want to do something meaningful? If you're asking about a relationship, what inspires you about that person?

2. What challenges you?

What do you find difficult, even frightening? What in that relationship bothers you, makes you want to hold back? Or maybe this card presents a challenge you would like to take on.

3. What doorway opens for you?

This is the crucial card. What opportunity presents itself to you? What could be different if you took a chance?

4. What will you risk?

Opportunities always carry some element of risk. A new job, a new relationship—these are wonderful, but think of all we could lose. Suppose in a relationship reading that position 4 shows the Hermit. You risk the Hermit sense of controlling your own life if you enter the relationship. This position doesn't

tell you what to do—it doesn't even say you will defi-
nitely lose something—it just shows what might be
different.

5. *What can you discover?*

What might happen if you went through that door?
This card can give a kind of snapshot of how your
life might look. The World might offer great success,
but suppose the Devil came up? Would you turn
back from whatever it was you were contemplating?
Maybe the Devil says going through the doorway
would reveal some long-standing problem, and it is
time to liberate yourself.

Dr. Apollo's All-Purpose Spread

Here is another five-card spread that many people have
found valuable. Dr. Apollo is a character I invented once for
a workshop in which I led people to create theatrical, magical
fortuneteller identities. I wanted a dramatic spread, something
you might use in a carnival setting. The result was something
a number of readers have said they indeed use for all their
readings.

Lay the cards out in the following manner:

1

3   5   4

2

Here are the "questions." Notice the exclamation points; Dr. Apollo urges us to take a dramatic approach.

1. *Known!*

This is something the querent knows but needs to look at more closely.

2. *Unknown!*

Here we find something the querent does not know but needs to learn.

3. *Danger!*

Something the querent needs to be very careful about.

4. *Opportunity!*

Here is something beneficial or powerful that can come from this situation.

5. *Action!!*

Where most modern readings do not tell us what to do, Dr. Apollo does not shy away from giving us a solid recommendation. Perhaps you can see why people like this spread!

The Celtic Cross

This is the most famous Tarot spread in the world, appearing in Waite's book and reprinted, with various modifications, countless times.

While the structure is almost always the same, the order (for example, which position comes third) varies according to different authors. The order I use comes originally from Eden Gray.

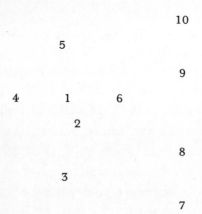

Card 1 goes in the center of the cross. It describes the overall issue or situation. Some call this the "cover" card (from Waite's statement, "This covers him").

Card 2 goes horizontally across the first. Traditionally people have seen this as "opposition," some force that goes against the first. In fact, the two may work together. We sometimes refer to the first two cards as the "small cross."

Card 3 goes below the first two and represents the "root" of the issue. Usually it shows some past experience or life history that influences the present.

Card 4, on the left side of the small cross, also shows the past, but it's a more "recent past," without deep roots. It may indicate something that is already over or fading away.

Card 5 goes above the small cross. People give different meanings to this position, but I find it helpful to think of it as "possibilities" and see it as the general way things are heading. If the "outcome" card ends up looking very different from the "possibilities," we can look at the other cards to see where the pattern shifts.

Card 6 shows the "near future." What will happen next in this situation? We need to remember that this card usually shows a temporary state. If it's good, make the best of it. If it's a problem, know that it won't last.

We read the four cards on the right, the "staff," from the bottom to the top. Card 7 shows "self," some way the querent her- or himself has contributed to the situation. Card 8 represents "others," the impact of other people. This card can show the influence of a single figure, such as a partner, or the general environment. In readings about career, I tend to look at this card as the economic situation (say, job prospects) beyond the person's control.

Card 9 concerns "hopes and fears." It's sometimes very valuable for the person to realize that it shows an attitude, a fantasy, not what is actually happening or will happen (unless the other cards support it).

Finally we come to card 10, the "outcome." This last card doesn't mean a prediction so much as a result of all the previous influences. We can examine what it shows us and try to see just how the root, the self, the recent past, and the rest end up moving in this direction. This is not an absolute prediction.

It just says, "This is where things are heading." We can use what we learn from the other cards to change something we don't like or to help along something we want to see happen.

Loving the Image

I have used these words to describe my approach to Tarot for over forty years. Despite all the millions of words written about Tarot, all the absolute statements, the cards remain, above all, pictures. To love the image means to try and look at it with fresh eyes every time it comes up. How does it look today—what is it showing you, telling you, right now? A good approach is to pick up a card in a reading and, instead of immediately trying to figure out what it says, see what detail catches your eye. Is it the Hermit's hand as he holds the lantern? The eagle's head on the Fool's bag? Maybe it's the ripples of water on the right side of the boat in the Six of Swords.

If these details could speak, what might they say to you? When you read for someone else, ask where they might see themselves in the picture. This can be especially valuable in cards with different characters, such as the Five of Swords or the Six of Pentacles.

Let yourself read the Tarot as an act of love.

· · · · · ·